44 5

"I am so glad that my dad has taken the time to compile some of the life-changing stories and lessons he has gained from his more than 45 years of ministry leadership. Using ancient illustrations from the Bible and personal successes and challenges from his own leadership, he will show you that some of the frustrating—even seemingly unconquerable—relational and professional struggles you are currently facing are both common to humankind and very conquerable.

"In fact, in the 20-plus years I have served with my dad, I personally have observed countless pastors and leaders—including myself—apply these principles to their lives to experience very significant and impactful change. Are you ready to conquer some of the relational and professional hindrances that have been holding you back? Read *Rise Up!* and learn from someone who not only has encountered these hindrances for decades, but who also clearly and applicably shares wise perspective and time-tested principles to overcome them."

—Pastor Jason Bolin

"In Acts 16, Paul's ministry was disrupted by what sounded to others like confirmation of his ministry. The apostle knew something wasn't right. It wasn't a psychological or personality issue. Through sensitive, spiritual discernment and wisdom, the disturbance was halted. Have you ever wondered what is hindering the success of the ministry to which you have been called? Gleaning from decades of pastoral ministry experience, Bishop Jim Bolin shares in this powerful book what he has encountered and successfully overcome by faith in God's Word!

"In this book and workbook, the author helps the twenty-first-century pastor understand how spiritual issues can create intense psychological stress and disrupt relationships in a church to the point that it impedes moving forward with the pastor's God-inspired vision. At the completion of this study, the student will have discovered a clear and concise strategy for victory. It is biblical and applicable!

"Bishop Bolin is a dear personal friend, and from time to time over the past 30 years, we have shared pulpits. I know this brother's heart is to help pastors fulfill the God-inspired visions in their places of ministry.

"This is your opportunity to learn from an experienced apostle—to learn biblical principles for defeating whatever it is hindering you. I believe in this message!"

—Dr. Jeff Burrell, Pastor, Zion Christian Assembly

"The book of Hosea teaches us that we can be destroyed because of what we do not know. It's possible that the work God wants to do in our lives could be hindered all because of unknown demonic forces. If there is anyone qualified to speak on this subject, it is Jim Bolin. My family and church have been receiving from this general for over two decades, and we are much better for it. I believe that, as you take the journey of reading and applying this life lesson, you will experience an unprecedented flow of the Holy Spirit and your life will be changed forever!"

—Sr. Pastor Richie Mullis, Free Life Church, Forney, TX

"No other resource will aid a pastor in the shaping and reformation of a church culture like *Rise Up!* Its sound biblical insights and practical applications are invaluable to the Kingdom, especially in this moment in time."

—P. Brien Sturgill, Pastor Sixth Avenue Church of God

"I highly recommend *Rise Up!* to any pastor, elder, deacon, or layperson who wants to understand what is hindering their church from growing and going to the next level. As a lead pastor, this book has been one of the most influential and useful books in my library. I have taken my congregation and leadership team through this material on two different occasions. The first time, as a newly appointed pastor, I needed to understand the spiritual dynamics of my new assignment. The second time, I went through it as an established pastor who felt his church was stuck. In both cases, the Holy Spirit used *Rise Up!* to open our eyes to the real hindrances that were blocking the flow of God's blessings. Once we identified, addressed, and removed those hindering spirits, our church experienced a fresh visitation of God's grace and glory!"

—Kenneth E. Angel, MA, Lead Pastor North Elliott
Street Church of God Pryor, Oklahoma

"This book, *Rise Up!*, reveals a life-changing revelation that takes solid biblical principles and puts them into a practical and useful strategy to release a spiritual revival in your church, ministry, and personal life. Every pastor should be required to read this book!"

Dr. Scott Hannen
Christian Television host and author of the best-selling
books, *Healing by Design* and *Stop the Pain!*

PREVIOUSLY PUBLISHED WORKS BY DR. JIM L. BOLIN:

The Rope of Hope: Strength for When You're Hanging by a Thread

How To Treat Your Kids Like God Treats His
written with Dr. Justin Harley

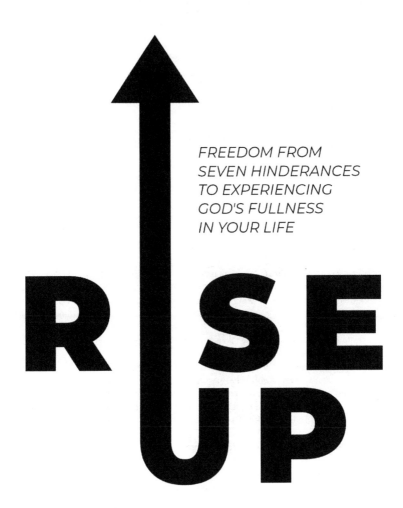

FREEDOM FROM
SEVEN HINDERANCES
TO EXPERIENCING
GOD'S FULLNESS
IN YOUR LIFE

RISE UP

JIM BOLIN

DREAM
RELEASER
PUBLISHING

For foreign and subsidiary rights, contact the author.

Cover design by: Sara Young
Author photo on cover: Michael Packer, Seven Springs Media

ISBN: 978-1-957369-40-2   1 2 3 4 5 6 7 8 9 10

Printed in the United States of America

Contents

ACKNOWLEDGEMENTS

I would like to dedicate this book to the love of my life, my wife, Robin. Thank you for standing with me during the difficult days and for believing in me even when I couldn't see my way forward. Most of all, thank you for loving me and covering me with your prayers.

I would also like to dedicate this book to my son, Jason, for his constant love, support, and encouragement; to his wife and my dear daughter-in-law, Sarah; to my precious and always-encouraging daughter, Jessica; and to my four awesome grandkids, Jay, Caroline, Berkleigh, and Jocelyn. Thanks for standing with Dad/Papa and allowing our lives to be a proving ground for the loving, forgiving, and accepting power of God.

I want to thank Dr. Justin Harley for his contribution of time, resources, and wisdom in dealing with the many facets of conflict in human nature. Your professional insights proved to be more valuable than I ever imagined.

I know I never could have accomplished victory in so many areas without a pastoral staff that loves and believes in me. Thanks to all members, and friends, of the congregation of Seven Springs that have stood with me through it all! I love you all!

FOREWORD

When tasked with the assignment of bringing order to the houses of God in which I have pastored, I have turned to and launched church-wide Bible studies using the insightful book written by Bishop Jim Bolin entitled *Rise Up! Freedom from Seven Hindrances to Experiencing God's Fullness in Your Life*. This book is written from the heart of a visionary leader, pastor, and veteran of many spiritual battles.

As a choice servant, this man of God has shared from his profound experience and biblical knowledge, in a manner that is empowering and beneficial to both persons in ministry and those in the pews. With revelatory insight, Bishop Bolin has revealed and exposed the many spirits that rage behind the numerous battles and attacks that the enemy has launched against kingdom builders, and explained how God has equipped us not only to survive, but to walk in victory over such spirits and attacks. I am convinced that this book is a must-read for both experienced ministers and beginners who have been called to engage in ministry.

I am extremely blessed to have shared decades of deep friendship, camaraderie, and ministry with this anointed kingdom general. Being a pastor of a multicultural ministry myself, he has blessed me as a confidant, advisor, and brother in Christ, and I am honored to highly recommend this Holy-Spirit-inspired book, which I am confident will bless you.

—Bishop William A. Lee, Jr.
Lead Pastor, Victorious Life Church
Conyers, Georgia

PREFACE

In 1983, we began Trinity Chapel—now known as Seven Springs Church—with fewer than fifty people. Despite all of my big dreams, I never expected to be pastoring a church of several thousand members while quickly seeking ways to accommodate the many more who were to come. When any pastor/leader experiences this growth in ministry, it is easy for others around him to misunderstand the process he went through to get where he is today.

Pastors and leaders often visit our church and ask us, "To what do you attribute your tremendous growth and success in ministry?" They see the growth with which we have been blessed, but often they cannot see the history of sacrifices we made in the process of achieving that growth. The battles we have been through and the conflicts we continue to face are tough, but the great things God is doing among us make the struggle and pain worthwhile.

What God has done in my life and ministry has been beyond my wildest imagination, but it has been a process. Through this process, I have faced many situations that seemed insurmountable; but with the Holy Spirit's help, I continue to come through them victoriously. I am not successful today because I have had a trouble-free life and ministry; I am blessed because God has led me to overcome each obstacle that hinders His presence and power from operating in my life, family, and ministry. I have personally dealt with the behaviors that cause division on countless occasions in my many years of service as a pastor.

I am only too well-acquainted with the murderous behavior that rips lives apart. I have had to deal with gossipers on hundreds of occasions. I know the pain that criticism causes, and I have been the object of its abuse. I also know that people who gossip can severely hurt a church if they are not dealt with properly. I have seen the divisive behavior of rebellion, and I know what it is like when someone you love and trust leads a rebellion against you. I have seen the selfish, greedy operation of erroneous behavior. I have witnessed the division brought on by disloyalty.

I have watched people as they exercised controlling behaviors in an attempt to manipulate me. I have been tempted to use my influence to manipulate others. Confusion and disorder have twisted my words and actions in order to incriminate me and confound our congregation.

Most of all, I have had to fight legalistic behavior in others. As a pastor, I have had to decide whether to impose legalism upon the people under my leadership. I have fought that temptation and continue to win the battle! I have had to deal with those who want to drag traditionalism back into our ministry, but now I'm better equipped to deal with legalistic behavior. Through all these trials, I have become stronger as a person, and our church has become a better place in which to serve and worship God. If I had not taken on the responsibility of dealing with these divisive behaviors, we would not have been able to reach the victorious place we now enjoy as a church.

My prayer is that you will use the concepts and wisdom in this book to identify areas of your life that are keeping you from becoming everything God has called you to be. You do not have to repeat the same struggles all your life. You can break free from these divisive behaviors.

However, if you do not learn to identify them, they will continue to plague you.

I pray what is shared with you in this book will keep you from fighting the same battles I have had to fight. I also pray this book will help you identify the deterrents to personal growth in your life and help you break through those patterns and barriers. May God reveal to you the behaviors that cause division in your life so that you may recognize them, overcome them, and live in victory, peace, and the joy of the Holy Spirit.

INTRODUCTION

Yet these people slander whatever they do not understand, and the very things they do understand by instinct—as irrational animals do—will destroy them. Woe to them! They have taken the way of Cain; they have rushed for profit into Balaam's error; they have been destroyed in Korah's rebellion.
—Jude 1:10-11 (NIV)

I n God's Word, we find at least seven behaviors that can hinder His operation in our lives. These behaviors are often present in your family, at your job, in your church, and wherever else you go. They can create division, distraction, and confusion. When you allow these behaviors to operate, they will hinder you from experiencing God's presence and power. The behaviors discussed in this book are not an exhaustive list, but an introduction to many of the battles I have worked through in my journey as a follower of Jesus and as a pastor.

As a senior pastor, I have witnessed firsthand the cruelty of these seven behaviors operating through people, and the pain and destruction that can result. Their effects are truly damaging to the body of Christ, and once they begin to operate and manifest, they can spread like cancer through any organization or group of people.

Many churches, families, and businesses are in trouble because they lack understanding about deep dynamics and forces at work within the organization. Keep in mind that, as bad as you want to succeed, you have an enemy who wants you to fail. In John 10:10a (NIV), Jesus tells us "The thief comes only to steal and kill and destroy." His plan for your life is to bring pain, sickness, hurt, sorrow, regret, fear, and any other detrimental thing that will keep you from realizing your full potential in Christ. If he can bring the opportunity for sin and pain into your life, he can hinder your potential to experience God's blessings.

We need to be aware of the schemes the enemy uses to try to harm us so that we can protect ourselves and help others too. The plan of the enemy is to entice us into engaging in behaviors that are contrary to God's Word—in other words, sinful—so he can hinder the blessing of God in our lives. A constant theological theme throughout the Bible is that God does not bless disobedience, nor does He curse righteousness (Galatians 6:4). Instead, God blesses obedience and curses disobedience (Deuteronomy 28–30). In Numbers 23 and 24, the children of Israel were immune to an evil curse until they opened a door by engaging in disobedience to God.

The enemy targets areas of your life, ministry, and business where he sees a weakness or an open door. Since he has no power on his own, he relies on finding areas in which, through strongholds or mindsets of disobedience, you have an exposure that allows him to attack. In Ephesians 4:27 (NIV), Paul tells us not to give the devil a foothold. Other versions of the same Scripture say not to give him a place or an opportunity. Over the next several chapters, you will read about behaviors that are contrary to the Word of God: that, if repeatedly engaged in, will give the devil an opportunity in your family or your church.

I understand that many people would rather focus on positive behaviors and avoid focusing on these pitfalls; but do not forget that the enemy is always waging a spiritual war against us, as we see in this Scripture:

For we do not wrestle against flesh and blood, but against principalities, against powers, against the rulers of the darkness of this age, against spiritual hosts of wickedness in the heavenly places.
—Ephesians 6:12 (NKJV)

Earlier in that same chapter of Ephesians, we are instructed to put on the full armor of God so we can take our stand against the devil's schemes.

There is good news. While the enemy is real and does exist, he is limited in time, space, and power. He is not the equal negative to God's positive and redemptive power, and he is not God! Jesus triumphed over the forces of evil, as Scripture says in Colossians 2:15 (NIV): "And having disarmed the powers and authorities, he made a public spectacle of them . . ."

In other words, Jesus stripped Satan of all his power. On the one hand, Satan is an old, toothless, clawless lion that can only roar at you and try to intimidate you into doing what he wants you to do. On the other hand, if you empower him to take advantage of a door you have opened in your life through doubt, fear, unbelief, and disobedience, he can cause destruction. If you do not allow him to come in, he cannot touch you. Knowing this fact, we can no longer blame all of our problems on the devil. Doors that we have opened in our lives through failing to submit to the will of God cause many of the problems with which we struggle.

As you read through the following chapters, I want you to first examine yourself. The temptation when reading about these divisive and destructive spirits is to think about other people that they might be operating in, allowing yourself to think poorly of someone else, or even flat-out going on a witch hunt. That is not the purpose of this book. The purpose of this book is to expose things the enemy may be using to try to hurt a church, or any group of people, and combat those things with God's Word so we can all walk in freedom. Just because a person demonstrates some of the characteristics I describe in this book, does not mean that this person is necessarily controlled by any particular spirit. We must use discernment and wisdom when helping someone work through a particular struggle. We must seek to love and serve others. We must remember that we are not struggling against people, but against spiritual forces at work. As Paul says in 1 Timothy 6:12, we must fight the good fight of faith. This battle is real and it is against real spirits! Wake up and realize that you are at war!

The following is a list of seven of the behaviors that can hinder the flow of God's presence and anointing in your life, your family, your business, and your ministry. These behaviors will be described in greater detail in the following chapters, but here is a brief overview.

CRITICISM

To criticize is to find fault with others. A critical spirit can always find the deficiencies, but it rarely finds the good. There are some strong analogies of criticism in the Bible, as we will see in the next chapter. We see this attitude in operation in Genesis 4, when Cain kills his brother Abel. The opposite of criticism is blessing and encouraging others.

REBELLION

To rebel is to oppose authority. All authority belongs to the Lord, but He delegates His authority to certain people at certain times. Rebelling against this authority is actually rebelling against God, and submitting to authority is submitting to God. We see this spirit in operation in the book of Numbers, when Korah turns against Moses. Rebellion, if not dealt with, is a dangerous spirit that can destroy any organization. When we submit to one another, we aren't submitting to a person—we are submitting to God's authority, which restores order.

ERROR

Error is the condition of being wrong. We see the spirit of error at work in Balaam when, due to his lack of understanding of God's truth, he tries to curse what God has already blessed. Today's culture, for the most part, denies the existence of right and wrong, truth and error. When you have no truth to stand on, this causes you to operate in error and you find yourself fighting against timeless principles that God has established. It also causes anxiety-provoking instability because you don't have a firm foundation of truth on which to stand. When you operate in the Spirit of Truth, you are cooperating with God's principles, setting yourself up for blessing.

DISLOYALTY

To be disloyal is to fail to honor your duties, obligations, and commitments to others. We see disloyalty in King David's son, Absalom. Unfortunately, Absalom failed to honor his father, the king of the nation. This happened at a time when his father needed him the most. Disloyalty fails to honor others, and therefore it fails to honor God. Think about how dangerous that is! When we operate in loyalty, we honor God and others.

CONTROL

To control someone is to try to influence them unfairly or manipulate them. We see control in operation in the spirit of Jezebel. Jezebel wasn't the leader of Israel, but she wanted to control the leader unfairly.

Jezebel's actions led the people's hearts away from the Lord to worship other gods, bringing disgrace and harm on the nation. Control undermines authority and therefore seeks to undermine God's plan. The counter to control is seeking to serve others. When we serve others, it restores God's order.

CONFUSION

Confusion is a lack of clarity. This spirit is mentioned in the books of Job and Isaiah as the twisted serpent, Leviathan. The enemy is constantly seeking to twist and pervert God's Word, turning people against God and against one another. When a spirit of confusion is at work, people cannot work in unity towards a common goal, and everything becomes much more difficult. When we have the mind of the Spirit, we have clarity, which helps restore unity in any group of people.

LEGALISM

Legalism is excessive adherence to a law or formula. We see legalism in operation in the Gospels in the spirit of the Pharisee. The Pharisee appears religious, but actually hinders people from being truly devoted to God with an overemphasis on rules and details. The opposite of legalism is freedom, and that freedom allows us to worship God without being weighed down by unnecessary burdens.

ARMING YOURSELF FOR BATTLE

While it is true that the enemy has a strategy to harm you, God has given you the necessary weapons to guard yourself against those attacks. 2 Corinthians 10:4-5 (NIV) says this:

> *The weapons we fight with are not the weapons of this world. On the contrary, they have divine power to demolish*

strongholds. We demolish arguments and every pretension that sets itself up against the knowledge of God, and we take captive every thought to make it obedient to Christ.

As you learn about the seven destructive behaviors, you will begin to expose areas in your life in which the enemy is attacking. You'll then be able to arm yourself with the power of Christ to resist these attacks. Do not try to come against any of these sins in the power of your own flesh. The Bible says to "be strong in the Lord and in his mighty power" (Ephesians 6:10, NIV). If you keep your eyes on the Lord and allow Him to lead you, He will begin to show you areas of your life where doors are open for an attack. Rely on the power of the Holy Spirit to keep you from the enemy.

Over the next few chapters, I want to go into detail on seven behaviors that hinder the presence and power of God in your life. Allow God to examine your heart to show you if any of these sins are active in you currently. Chances are that you will find one or more of them at work, trying to negate what you are doing for Christ. Examine your family: are there spiritual strongholds actively trying to rip you apart? At your workplace, how many of these behaviors are present? When you engage in social media, how many of these behaviors have you allowed to slip in? Most importantly, which sins are hindering you from becoming everything God has called you to be? You will find that these sins are present in all

> Most importantly, which sins are hindering you from becoming everything God has called you to be?

walks of life. You may have battled with them all your life and not even come to terms with exactly what they are. I hope this book helps you to identify them so that you can break the barriers holding you back from becoming the person God has called you to be.

Journey with me as we examine the behaviors that cause division in your life. We will learn how they take root, how to identify them, and how to begin to correct them. Once we correct the behaviors that limit God's power in our lives, we can open up doors for His power to operate without hindrance.

NAME	SCRIPTURAL EXAMPLE	COUNTER
Criticism	Cain – Genesis 4	Blessing
Rebellion	Korah – Numbers 16	Submission
Error	Balaam – Numbers 22	Truth
Disloyalty	Absalom – 2 Samuel 15	Loyalty
Control	Jezebel – 1 Kings 16	Servanthood
Confusion	Leviathan – Job 41	Clarity
Legalism	The Pharisees – Matthew 23	Freedom

CHAPTER ONE

FROM CRITICISM TO BLESSING

Can both fresh water and salt flow from the same spring?
—James 3:11 (NIV)

I grew up in Pasadena, California, but as a child, I loved going on trips to visit my extended family in Mississippi and Arkansas. In the late fifties, most houses in the country had electricity, but not plumbing. One of my favorite things to do while away was going to the outhouse. For some reason, I thought this was fun when I was a kid. When you are a kid growing up in Pasadena, you do not have the *privilege* of going outside to use the bathroom. If we used the bathroom in the backyard at home, Momma would have slapped us silly. But when we were away, it was okay.

Another treat we did not get in Pasadena was drinking water from a well. Some of the best-tasting water I have ever had was fresh, cold water from those wells.

Imagine what your response would be if you went to a well to get water and, when you began to drink, you got a mouthful of saltwater. This is exactly the illustration the book of James gives us about the words we choose:

> *Out of the same mouth come praise and cursing. My brothers and sisters, this should not be. Can both fresh water and salt water flow from the same spring? My brothers and sisters, can a fig tree bear olives, or a grapevine bear figs? Neither can a salt spring produce fresh water.*
> —James 3:10-12 (NIV)

WHAT IS A CRITICAL SPIRIT?

To criticize is to express disapproval of someone based on perceived faults or mistakes. I will admit that there is such a thing as constructive criticism—and it can be very helpful; but people who struggle with a critical spirit can find fault in just about anyone and anything. In addition, they often have a difficult time finding the good in others. Have you ever heard the saying that there is a silver lining in every cloud? Well, for those who struggle with a critical spirit, there is a cloud in every silver lining.

Like most of the behaviors listed in this book, a critical spirit is rooted in pride. Although pride has many definitions, the definition I am referring to is the belief that you are somehow better than other people. If I believe I am better than others, I will see and magnify their faults while minimizing my own. A critical spirit, like the other behaviors in this book, starts in the heart. It starts with a belief that other people are no better than me, and maybe I am better than them. As Jesus teaches, these beliefs in our heart defile us.

The words we speak reflect what is in our hearts. If your heart is full of bad stuff, bad stuff will come out. You may be able to bite your tongue for a while, but if you really want to change your speech, you must change it from the inside out. Jesus said, "For out of the abundance of the heart the mouth speaks" (Matthew 12:34b, NKJV).

> The words we speak reflect what is in our hearts.

A critical spirit leads to negative thoughts and feelings like anger, jealousy, competition, selfish ambition, and the like. We spew hatred, slander, gossip, and backbiting remarks out of our mouths, all intended to hurt others and pull them down. At the same time, we keep ourselves lifted up.

Because of our need to be included, loved, and admired, we often seek to tear others down so that they will respect us. We falsely believe that, if we expose others' flaws, people will view us as "normal." The desire to criticize others, therefore, often begins in our hurts, inadequacies, and insecurities. As you continue to read, you will learn ways to address these insecurities.

BIBLICAL EXAMPLE: CAIN KILLS ABEL

Interpersonal conflict is nothing new. It goes back to the beginning of humanity. We see it in the relationship between the first two siblings, Cain and Abel. To say that Cain had a problem would be an understatement. Cain did not decide to kill his brother out of the blue. What was so wrong with him that caused him to kill? He did it because of deep-seated emotions of anger and jealousy that had been stirring inside of him. God loved Abel's offering, but he did not receive Cain's because Cain knew the kind of offering that was to be brought but didn't bring it.

Have you ever worked hard at something only to see someone else get the credit? I imagine that is what Cain felt like. I imagine he asked himself the question, "Why did God accept Abel and not me?" Yet if you study the story, you will find that Abel was a keeper of the flock and Cain was a tiller of the soil. Cain dug, weeded, planted, pruned, and gathered the harvest. I am sure that he worked hard. Just like Martha and Mary in the New Testament, Cain was working while Abel was worshiping. The bottom line is this: Cain did not worship God in the right way. The fruit of the ground was acceptable for tithes, but not as a covering for one's sins. Abel's offering was accepted because he worshiped according to the pattern that God had given him, while Cain did not.

Immediately following Cain's abominable act, God asked him, "Why are you angry? Why is your face downcast?" (Genesis 4:6b, NIV)

A critical spirit always starts with a thought. Once this thought takes root, it begins to grow and, just like in Cain, a spirit of murder can be conceived. Notice who Cain murdered: his own flesh and blood! Imagine murdering your own family. Critical spirits are unfortunately wreaking havoc on churches in our country. People even take to social media to publicly lambast one another—and their own families at that! Maybe they don't attack their biological family (although that does happen), but they will attack their church family. This should not be!

The Spirit of God spoke through Paul to tell the believers that they were biting and devouring each other (Galatians 5:15). These are strong words. When we talk negatively about each other, it is as if we are biting and devouring each other. When we operate from a critical spirit, we figuratively—but in a relational way—bite and chew each other up and spit each other out. When we do this, we are guilty of *spiritual cannibalism.* We are consuming each other. Does this sound gross? It is gross—and it is a sin.

Spiritually speaking, the apostle John adds that anyone who hates his brother in his heart is guilty of murder (1 John 3:15). You do not have to take a knife to someone to commit murder, nor do you have to get a gun and shoot someone. In a way, we murder one another every single day through our thoughts, attitudes, and words.

We have all been guilty of a critical spirit. In this chapter, we will examine how this destructive spirit infiltrates the lives of believers in order to tear them apart.

IDENTIFYING A CRITICAL SPIRIT

As stated earlier, a critical spirit can easily find fault and identify the problems and shortcomings of others. A critical spirit finds fault in nearly everything that happens within a church. A critical spirit says, *"It is too hot." "It is too cold." "It is too loud." "It is not loud enough."*

When people come into a church, they are often hurting and looking for love, acceptance, and forgiveness. They need someone to extend mercy to them, just as the Lord has extended mercy to us all. Too many times, instead of finding a place of mercy, people get ripped apart by a critical spirit. This critical spirit wears people down. The Bible says we are supposed to "edify," or build others up (1 Thessalonians 5:11); but when we're operating from a critical spirit, we tear each other down.

THE DEVASTATING EFFECTS OF A CRITICAL SPIRIT

The thoughts and attitudes Cain harbored in his heart against his brother Abel had devastating results. Likewise, a critical spirit, left unchecked, is catastrophically destructive. Have you ever heard the saying, "Sticks and stones may break my bones, but words will never hurt me"? Whoever said that missed it. Words *do* hurt. They hurt others, but they hurt the one who says them even more.

A critical spirit tears others down. As Christ-followers, we are supposed to be giving life to others. A critical spirit is like a drain that sucks the life and energy out of others. You can either be a fountain of blessing or you can be a drain. Be a fountain!

A critical spirit damages our credibility. If we spend all our energy finding one another's faults, we fail to bring God glory by bringing glory to His church. A critical spirit damages our reputation, it creates division, and it negates all that is positive in your life. It creates division in organizations. But it doesn't just hurt others—it hurts you too.

> People are made in the image of God. Slanderous remarks about others are slanderous remarks about God.

When it comes to the words you speak, you can be confident that you reap what you sow. If you expect good things to come to you, you had better start sending some good things out. Listen to Proverbs

18:21 (NIV): "The tongue has the power of life and death, and those who love it will eat its fruit."

One way or another, you will experience the return of the words you sow with your tongue. If you constantly criticize others, you will reap a bitter harvest. If you practice encouraging people and loving them, you will find a harvest of righteousness in return. If you say you love God but hate your neighbor, the Bible calls you a liar (1 John 4:20). If you truly love people, you will not spend time trying to find fault with them and destroying them with your mouth. In addition, people are made in the image of God (Genesis 1:27). Slanderous remarks about others are slanderous remarks about God.

We will give an account for every vain, careless, and judgmental word we speak. Our words do not die after we speak them. They live on, recorded in the annals of history—and, at times, the internet. When you catch yourself speaking negatively about others, understand that you will give an account to God for every word (Matthew 12:36-37). Not only that, but your words either make you or break you. They will justify you or condemn you. The Bible does not say that you will be justified or condemned by the way you dress, an alcohol or cigarette addiction, the position that you hold, how much of the Bible you can quote, or anything else. You will be justified or condemned by your words.

It does not matter how spiritual you think you are or how much of the Bible you can quote—if you cannot control your speech, you become toxic to others and to yourself. Until you bring what you say into line with God's Word, your religion is worthless.

James 1:26 (NIV) states, "Those who consider themselves religious and yet do not keep a tight rein on their tongues deceive themselves, and their religion is worthless."

Likewise, James writes this later in his letter:

> *With the tongue we praise our Lord and Father, and*
> *with it we curse human beings, who have been made in*
> *God's likeness. Out of the same mouth come praise and*
> *cursing. My brothers and sisters, this should not be.*
> —James 3:9-10 (NIV)

You can damage a person's reputation without a single word—with just a look or a facial expression. Sometimes, it is not what you say but how you "speak" with the rest of your body. David writes this in Psalm 62:3-4 (NIV):

> *How long will you assault me? Would all of you throw me*
> *down—this leaning wall, this tottering fence? Surely they intend*
> *to topple me from my lofty place; they take delight in lies. With*
> *their mouths they bless, but in their hearts they curse.*

Be careful how you speak to those in your family and those over whom you have influence. It is reported that it takes seven positive words to neutralize one negative word spoken. People call churches and other organizations every day to seek counseling, and a major reason they make those calls is because, for their entire lives, they've had someone destroying them with negative words. Work hard to build up your family and you will receive a harvest for your efforts.

Before we move on to the last part of recognizing the divisiveness of criticism, I would be foolish not to address what I call the "gossip passer." These individuals receive gossip or criticism about another individual without holding the person who is speaking accountable. "Gossip passers" are part and party to the spirit of murder. James 3:5 (NIV) says, "Likewise, the tongue is a small part of the body, but it makes great boasts. Consider what a great forest is set on fire by a small spark."

When we receive a negative report about someone else without them being present or without knowing the facts—when we retweet something negative about someone else or share a post simply to gossip or point fingers—we are just as guilty as the one speaking the poison. As I heard Pastor John Hagee say one time, "If you're not an eyewitness, you're a false witness."

Conversely, we can perpetuate the flow of God's goodness by speaking the truth in love. Words of encouragement can bring peace to any situation.

TURNING CRITICISM INTO BLESSING

Just as words can be destructive, they also have great healing power. Words start wars, but they also end wars. The opposite of a critical spirit is a spirit that blesses and encourages others. We should all seek to develop this spirit of encouragement in our lives, and we can do this by the power of His Spirit.

If you want to stop criticizing others, you are going to need help. Have you ever said, "I am not going to talk bad about anybody ever again," and then turned around and done it? James 3:8 (NIV) says, "But no human being can tame the tongue. It is a restless evil, full of deadly poison."

Jesus is telling us that, if we have a problem with our tongue, we have a problem that runs deep. James writes and asks,

Does a spring send forth fresh water and bitter from the same opening? Can a fig tree, my brethren, bear olives, or a grapevine bear figs? Thus no spring yields both salt water and fresh.
—James 3:11-12 (NKJV)

Just as Cain did the evil that he harbored in his heart, your speech will reflect the good or evil that is in your heart.

The remedy to negative speech is to allow God to put a bridle on you and a bit in your mouth (James 3:3). Since the tongue is a very hard muscle to control, we will need God's help to do this successfully. When the Bible speaks of a "bit," it is talking about listening to the voice of the Holy Spirit when He nudges you and tells you that what you are saying or doing is wrong. That is the time to listen and stop before you go any further. Bridling your tongue is not an option for the Christian. You *must* bridle your tongue. Only with God's help can you discover the way to control your tongue—what you say.

We find the answer to controlling the tongue in Isaiah 6. After God called Isaiah to be a prophet, he literally went off on the people of Israel, pronouncing woe after woe on them without ever addressing his own problems. But in chapter 6:5-7 (NIV), he says this:

> *"Woe to me!" I cried. "I am ruined! For I am a man of unclean lips, and I live among a people of unclean lips, and my eyes have seen the King, the Lord Almighty." Then one of the seraphim flew to me with a live coal in his hand, which he had taken with tongs from the altar. With it he touched my mouth and said, "See, this has touched your lips; your guilt is taken away and your sin atoned for."*

The first thing you must do to get control of your mouth is to seek and draw near to God. When you see God, you will see yourself for who you really are. Standing next to a holy God, the light of His radiant character shines into the darkness of your life. You realize the hidden places you have tried to keep secret. When you get into God's presence, you see the holiness of God and your speech begins to change.

Secondly, as we experience God's presence and we begin to see ourselves, we must repent. The angel touched the coal to Isaiah's lips and cleansed them. He became pure and was sent forth as God's anointed messenger. If you want to change your talk, make it your goal to get into God's presence and repent. Tell God that you were wrong. He will help you cleanse your speech and send you to give the kind of life-giving help people need. If you are prone to talking, texting, or sharing about others in a way you know is not right, ask God to forgive you and expect His help to overcome this stronghold in your life.

Lastly, we need to have a gate over our mouths. Here is what Psalm 141:3 (NIV) says: "Set a guard over my mouth, Lord; keep watch over the door of my lips."

Allen Redpath, who was one of the former pastors of Moody Church, Chicago, came up with a great acrostic a long time ago: THINK before you speak. Before you say something about someone else, ask yourself these five important questions:

T—Is it True? How many times does a rumor run rampant because someone repeated or retweeted something that simply was not true? Spreading false information is not godly. If the truth sets us free, then a lie keeps us in bondage. Why spread a lie that will have the potential to keep others from their freedom? Spreading false information also damages your credibility. Don't ever repeat anything that is not true. If you are not sure if it is true or not, use these three words: *verify, verify, verify.*

H—Is it Helpful? Just because something is true doesn't mean it is helpful. The apostle Paul says it best:

> *Do not let any unwholesome talk come out of your mouths,*
> *but only what is helpful for building others up according*
> *to their needs, that it may benefit those who listen.*

—Ephesians 4:29, NIV

I—Is it Inspiring? Words are powerful. They are an opportunity to bring life to others. As Proverbs 16:24 (KJV) says, "Pleasant words are as an honeycomb, sweet to the soul, and health to the bones."

N—Is it Necessary? We have all heard the saying that there is a reason God gave us two ears but only one mouth. There are numerous Scriptures that implore us to talk less, as this one does: "A gossip betrays a confidence; so avoid anyone who talks too much" (Proverbs 20:19, NIV).

K—Is it Kind? As 1 Corinthians 13:4 (NIV) says, "love is kind." You can offer constructive criticism to those around you—if done in a godly manner, the goal will be to build others up, not tear them down. So careful attention must be paid to the tone and manner of speech.

If you are struggling with your attitude and control over the words of your mouth, then pray this prayer with me:

Dear Father,

I come to You in the Name of Jesus and acknowledge my struggle with criticism. I have been exposed to the truth in Your Word about how the enemy tries to operate on or through me and I reject and renounce it today in Jesus' Name. Your Word also says that when I know Your truth, "the truth will set you free" (John 8:32, ESV). I receive the truth of Your Word today and declare that, "If the Son sets you free, you will be free indeed" (John 8:36, NIV), and by faith in Your finished work at Calvary, I AM FREE!

I pray now, fill me fresh with Your Spirit and wisdom to walk in this freedom and experience the joy You have designed for my life. Amen!

CHAPTER TWO

FROM REBELLION
TO SUBMISSION

*Korah son of Izhar, the son of Kohath, the son of Levi, and certain
Reubenites—Dathan and Abiram, sons of Eliab, and On son of
Peleth—became insolent and rose up against Moses. With them were
250 Israelite men, well-known community leaders who had been
appointed members of the council. . . . Then Moses summoned Dathan
and Abiram, the sons of Eliab. But they said, "We will not come! Isn't
it enough that you have brought us up out of a land flowing with milk
and honey to kill us in the wilderness? And now you also want to lord
it over us! Moreover, you haven't brought us into a land flowing with
milk and honey or given us an inheritance of fields and vineyards.
Do you want to treat these men like slaves? No, we will not come!"*
—Numbers 16:1-2, 12-14 (NIV)

once pastored a man who desperately wanted to sing on stage at
the church. I'm thankful for his eagerness to serve, but there were a

couple of problems: (1) he could not carry a tune in a bucket, and (2) he could not remember the words. He would get up, get less than halfway through the song, forget the words, and say "Bless God, I'm not going to let the devil stop me. Back it up and let's sing it again." I would sing along with him to try to help him remember the words. Despite his lack of giftedness in this area, he refused to accept the fact that he was out of place. No one could convince him otherwise, and he insisted that he keep singing in the choir and on the praise team.

Finally, one day, I had to sit him down, look him in the eyes, and say, "Look at me. You cannot sing. You can't carry a tune. You can make a joyful noise in the congregation, or at home in the shower, but you are not getting the microphone anymore." Those who know me know that I can say that type of a thing to a person with enough love and kindness that they usually receive it well.

He didn't. Instead, he tried to go around and gain support for his cause—or lack of ability. Thankfully, people knew I was right and helped put a quick end to his unwillingness to submit. I wish all rebellion were that easy to handle; but the truth is, often it can be devastating when left unattended.

WHAT IS REBELLION?

Simply put, to rebel is to oppose authority. When a person rebels, they do not want to submit to the authority that has been placed over them, nor do they want to operate in the order God has established. While the case of rebellion listed above probably seems mild, it is rebellious when someone tries to assume a position or remain in a position they were not called to or appointed to by proper leadership.

Various things cause a spirit of rebellion, but the root—as in all sin—is pride. It is human nature to look at another person and think, "They are not better than me." This thought process is dangerous and completely misses the point. All authority belongs to God.

Consider this Scripture: "Then Jesus came to them and said, 'All authority in heaven and on earth has been given to me'" (Matthew 28:18, NIV). The Lord delegates His authority to certain people at certain times. For example, the Lord delegates some of His authority to parents so they can raise their children—hopefully, in the ways of God. When authority is delegated, it does not cease to belong to the Lord; He simply allows us to steward it.

In a later chapter, we will discuss disloyalty. People who are disloyal, while still in the wrong, will often behave discreetly and subversively. People who rebel often do so openly. This causes deep division within a church. When we rebel against authority, we are not just rebelling against a person—we are rebelling against God Himself. This brings us back to pride. When you submit to authority, you are not admitting that a person is better than you; you are simply admitting that God is better than you. You are submitting to Him! You are stating that you believe that God is in charge and that you are willing to follow the order He has established.

KORAH'S REBELLION

In Numbers 16, Korah led 250 men in a spiritual and civil rebellion against Moses and Aaron. These 250 men had witnessed the miraculous deliverance of Israel from Egyptian slavery. These men stood at the edge of death as God parted the Red Sea and delivered them from the enemy. These men had witnessed God send manna from heaven. Yet they saw their current problems, blamed them on Moses' leadership, and wanted to forcefully and openly change the way things were being run.

What motivated Korah to incite this rebellion? If you look back into the third chapter of Numbers, the Bible reveals the initial opening of a door to rebellion in Korah's life. Korah, a man who led a national rebellion with 250 influential leaders, was not even chosen to lead his own tribe. Instead, he was passed up for the position in exchange for a younger man. He was trying to stand in a position to which God had not called him.

Korah went directly to Moses with his problem. He brought 250 of his friends to have a meeting with Moses and Aaron. Have you ever had a meeting called on you? In this meeting, they gave Moses a list of complaints against him that looked something like this:

→ You have too much authority.
→ You think you are the only holy one.
→ You lift yourself up above the congregation.
→ You brought us out of Egypt.
→ You make yourself a prince over us.
→ You have not given us an inheritance.
→ You keep none of your promises.

The list that we sometimes get as pastors looks like this:

→ We do not like the bushes on the side of the building.
→ There are a few light bulbs out in the sanctuary.
→ You preached past noon three Sundays in a row.
→ The music is too loud.
→ You authorized a $25 expense for steam-cleaning the church van without approval.

If you have never pastored, you may think I am kidding, but I am serious! In my many years of ministry experience, I have seen people get bent out of shape over some pretty ridiculous things. Rebellion causes people to stoop to absolutely asinine levels to find fault with people in authority, and it will leave you so blind that you fail to see the ignorance in which you function. It was a desire for recognition that caused Korah and his gang to rebel against Moses and Aaron.

IDENTIFYING A REBELLIOUS SPIRIT

People who rebel against authority often blame the leader for making bad decisions. It is true that ungodly or unfair leadership sometimes provokes people to rebel. There are numerous examples of this, such as the revolution that preceded the founding of the United States. When we are being led by someone, it is not an unusual occurrence to be hurt by decisions they make from time to time. Additionally, there is a tendency in people to resist boundaries and question the rules. However, just because a leader—like a pastor or staff member of a church—makes a decision you disagree with, does not mean you can start a revolution. God has established order, especially in His church. When you have a disagreement, there are proper, godly, and biblical ways to handle these types of situations. The godly way to handle it is not to openly oppose the one God has placed over you for that time. Unless someone leading you is directly threatening your life or physical safety, rebellion is dangerous to your spiritual health, and hinders the blessing of God in your life.

> Rebellion is dangerous to your spiritual health, and hinders the blessing of God in your life.

As a pastor, I have seen people allow rebellion to operate within them because they felt left out or overlooked. If you aren't careful, the desire for recognition will cause pride to swell up in your heart. You will start to question every decision the leader makes. This is exactly what happened with Korah and the other men who rebelled against Moses. They saw what seemed like questionable or even poor decisions, and started thinking they could lead the nation better than Moses could.

It is easy to feel like you have been overlooked, or to believe that you are more gifted than a certain person who has a position you want. You may begin believing that you could preach better than the preacher, sing better than the worship leader, play better than the band, lead better than the leader, or boss better than the boss. When this happens, the spirit of rebellion creeps into your heart. Even if you *could* lead better than the leader, if God has not called you to do it, then you are out of place. When we despise authority, we are in essence saying to God, "Why did you put them in leadership instead of me? You do not know what you are doing!" People in authority rule because God put them there. Your pastor is at your church because God placed him there. Your boss is at your company because God placed him or her there. If you could do so much better, why didn't God make you the pastor, the CEO, the top leader? When you question the authority of others, you begin to question God's authority.

Often, when people rebel, they also try to take over. Maybe they try to take over the whole church, the board, or some other position of authority or influence. When a person tries to take over and operate in a position in which they have not been properly placed, it becomes rebellion. Many times, they will try to disguise what they're doing and hide behind something that appears to be spiritual. Such was the case with Korah.

It is impossible for one person's rebellion to affect just them. When rebellion begins to grow in someone's heart, it can ultimately affect the whole church, business, nation, or family. Korah began by feeling neglected and overlooked, and recruited 250 leaders to rebel with him. Before long, the rebellion had spread throughout the entire camp. Because God's judgment broke out against them, almost 15,000 people died during this incident (Numbers 16:49). If Aaron had not gone to the altar and made a sacrifice when he did, many more would have perished. Do you see how destructive rebellion is?

Rebellion is never a solitary act. It can tear apart a whole church. How many times have we witnessed someone getting angry in church or in a business and, before they leave, getting on the phone and calling the elders, the staff, and anyone else who might listen? Maybe they post comments on social media about the "breakup," egging people on to agree with them, searching for sympathizers, and pulling people's heartstrings. Rebellious people often want to do as much damage as they can to the leader because they somehow feel the leader has hurt them, and they want to retaliate. Rarely will a rebellious person leave quietly without making a big stink. What they do not know is that the same dilemma may await them at their next church or place of employment.

OVERCOMING REBELLION WITH SUBMISSION

If you are the pastor of a church or a leader in ministry, recognize your authority but do not abuse it. This authority was delegated to you by Jesus for you to be a faithful steward of discipleship development. In 2 Chronicles 26, King Uzziah stands as one of the greatest kings in Israel's history. He was responsible for the rebuilding of the nation, as well as technological advancements that solidified their army as a formidable foe. His tragic flaw was his pride. The Bible reveals that he began to think more highly of himself than he ought. He abused his authority by offering incense in the temple of God. He stepped above what God had appointed him to do. When spiritual leaders begin to abuse their authority, God knows how to take them down. Uzziah was stricken with leprosy, and was forced to live outside of the community until he died.

While we must make sure we do not abuse our authority, we must also understand as leaders that God has delegated authority to us—as long as we stay submitted to Him. That means that, at times, we must lovingly deal with the spirit of rebellion by helping people understand that authority belongs to God, and we must honor the order He has established.

Helping others understand the need to respect the authority God has set in place will help the church fall into line with God's order and will. If people do not respect authority, they will be subject to the detrimental effects of the spirit of rebellion.

Ephesians 4:11-16 (NIV) states:

> *So Christ himself gave the apostles, the prophets, the evangelists, the pastors and teachers, to equip his people for works of service, so that the body of Christ may be built up until we all reach unity in the faith and in the knowledge of the Son of God and become mature, attaining to the whole measure of the fullness of Christ. Then we will no longer be infants, tossed back and forth by the waves, and blown here and there by every wind of teaching and by the cunning and craftiness of people in their deceitful scheming. Instead, speaking the truth in love, we will grow to become in every respect the mature body of him who is the head, that is, Christ. From him the whole body, joined and held together by every supporting ligament, grows and builds itself up in love, as each part does its work.*

To rebel is to openly oppose authority. To submit is to yield to the authority of another person. Learn to close the door of rebellion in your life by loving and submitting to one another. The answer to rebellion is found in Ephesians: "love one another" (4:2) and "submit to one another" (5:21). When you do those two things, you have peace with authority so that the work of the kingdom may be accomplished. Most babies are not created out of a hateful fight. Babies are made out of love and intimacy between a man and a woman. If we begin to love one another and submit to one another in the family of God, we can give birth to many great things.

As stated earlier, yielding to someone else's leadership is not an admission that they are smarter than you, better than you, or more powerful than you. Yielding to authority simply admits that you want to honor the Lord, the order He has established, and the people He has placed in your life.

If you want to remain under the covering of spiritual authority, you must understand the reason God has placed people in authority. Authority is a good thing. God has established authority not to harm us but to help us. Men and women who abuse authority are the ones who bring hurt, not God. If you find a man or woman in authority who is after the heart of God, submitting to that authority will ultimately draw you closer to God and allow you to experience His blessings in your life.

> Authority is a good thing. God has established authority not to harm us but to help us.

However, if a man or woman in authority is not seeking God, that does not give you the right to turn on them, undermine their authority, or try to bring harm to them. Guard that person and protect them. Pray for the Holy Spirit to open up an opportunity to speak to the person in authority; and if that doesn't happen, then continue to pray and know the Holy Spirit is handling it His way. Do not allow the devil to justify rebellion against authority by showing you flaws in the life of a leader.

There is an awesome benefit to submitting to God's authority: you come under the umbrella of His protection. Since God has placed authority in your life to protect you and to draw you closer to Him, submitting to it invokes a special protection from Him. Therefore, support your leaders, regardless of whether they are wrong or right. Love them when they are right and love them when they are wrong. Love them when they step up to the plate and hit a home run, and love them when they strike out. If you come to a point where you can no longer keep your mouth shut and pray for them, then get out! But do not take others with you. That scheme is the spirit of rebellion manifesting. Do not say, "I am out of here and I am going to bring this ship down with me!" Talk about bringing the wrath of God in your life! The earth opened up and swallowed Korah and his devilish clan. What do you think will happen in your life if you try to undermine someone in authority over you?

To head off the spirit of rebellion, consider what you might do to make the life of one of your leaders easier. This type of service is holy and pleasing to God. Begin by creating a mental list of things that you can do to assist your pastor, supervisor, parents, or other authorities. Begin performing these actions as a service to God. If rebellion initiated the wrath of God, causing the earth to open up and swallow people, submitting to one another will surely invite the blessings of God upon your life!

First Timothy 5:17 (NIV) says, "The elders who direct the affairs of the church well are worthy of double honor, especially those whose work is preaching and teaching." When you understand that blessing a man or woman of God brings a blessing into your life, you will not have any trouble blessing your pastor or other authority figures. Do not give your pastor what you consider a fair salary. Give him double that. When you loosen your grip on your pastors and bless them, God will bless your church. He will bless your businesses and jobs. I know your pastor is not perfect, and he does not have everything worked out. That does not matter. He has been laboring in the kingdom, and the Bible says that he deserves double honor. Paul also writes to the Church at Thessalonica and says,

And we urge you, brethren, to recognize those who labor among you, and are over you in the Lord and admonish you, and to esteem them very highly in love for their work's sake. Be at peace among yourselves.
—1 Thessalonians 5:12-13 (NKJV)

The spirit of rebellion is propagated by Satan to destroy the unity of the saints and to undermine God's established authority. In doing this, the enemy will stop the flow of God's blessing in our lives and our churches. Submit to God's authority. You are not submitting to a person. You are not admitting that anyone is better than you. You are only admitting that God is better than you. But when you rebel, you are rebelling against God, since all authority belongs to Him.

If you feel that a door is open in your life to rebellion, or you have already acted in a rebellious manner towards someone in authority over you, do not fall into the trap that Korah did. Pray this prayer now:

Dear Father,

I come to You in the Name of Jesus and acknowledge my struggle with rebellion. I have been exposed to the truth in Your Word about how the enemy tries to operate on or through me and I reject and renounce it today in Jesus' Name. Your Word also says that when I know Your truth, "the truth will set you free" (John 8:32, ESV). I receive the truth of Your Word today and declare that, "If the Son sets you free, you will be free indeed" (John 8:36, NIV), and by faith in Your finished work at Calvary, I AM FREE!

I pray now, fill me fresh with Your Spirit and wisdom to walk in this freedom and experience the joy You have designed for my life. Amen!

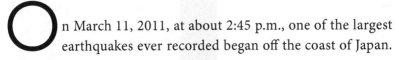

CHAPTER THREE

FROM ERROR TO TRUTH

God came to Balaam and asked, "Who are these men with you?"
Balaam said to God, "Balak son of Zippor, king of Moab, sent me this
message: 'A people that has come out of Egypt covers the face of the
land. Now come and put a curse on them for me. Perhaps then I will be
able to fight them and drive them away.'" But God said to Balaam, "Do
not go with them. You must not put a curse on those people, because
they are blessed."... Balaam got up in the morning, saddled his donkey
and went with the Moabite officials. But God was very angry when
he went, and the angel of the Lord stood in the road to oppose him.
—Numbers 22:9-12, 21-22 (NIV)

Woe to them!... they have rushed for profit into Balaam's error...
—Jude 11 (NIV)

On March 11, 2011, at about 2:45 p.m., one of the largest earthquakes ever recorded began off the coast of Japan.

Six minutes of intense shaking triggered a massive tsunami as well as thousands of intense aftershocks. Once it was all over, the entire island of Japan was moved eight feet to the east. The mass of the earth shifted so drastically that its axis was altered by four inches, which shortened each day by one microsecond. Also, 122,000 buildings had been completely destroyed, and over 300,000 more were damaged. The buildings were destroyed because the foundations underneath them shook so violently.

If we are going to weather the storms of life, we need a solid foundation on which to stand. One of the major challenges we are dealing with today is that the majority of young people do not believe in absolute truth. Instead, they believe in what is called moral relativity. Additionally, a lot of Christians—even pastors—no longer stand on the firm foundation of Scriptural truth. Major denominations are splitting and enduring legal battles because, it seems, half the leadership is holding to Biblical truths while the other half is not.

The Bible says that the church is built on the foundation of the apostles and prophets, with Jesus Christ Himself as the Chief Cornerstone (Ephesians 2:20). When we abandon beliefs that are foundational to our faith—beliefs taught by the apostles and prophets—we are messing with the foundation. I have done some renovations to my house before, but I have never thought about ripping out the foundation.

Studies show that anxiety levels in our country are absolutely off the charts right now. One reason for this is that many people don't have a firm foundation on which to stand. When you don't know what you believe in, there is nothing solid to stand on when the storms of life come. We need to hold firm to the foundations of God's truth so we can stand firm against the onslaught of error eroding our culture.

WHAT IS ERROR?

Error is the condition of being wrong. Today's culture, for the most part, denies the existence of right and wrong, truth and error. How can we make wise and just decisions if we deny the existence of truth? When you have no truth to stand on, this causes you to operate in error and you find yourself fighting against timeless principles that God has established.

BALAAM'S ERROR

Recorded in the Old Testament Book of Numbers chapters 22-24, the story of the prophet Balaam is one of much controversy. Many people believe Balaam was a slick, calculated soothsayer who knew how to manipulate words and people to achieve his own personal goals. Many believe Balaam only had the appearance of someone hearing from God. Upon careful examination of this story, you will find that, at one point, Balaam was an anointed prophet of God. Balaam heard the voice of God. He also knew what it meant to be in the presence of God. But Balaam began to rely on his flesh. He allowed what he felt to override what God was saying and doing in his spirit. Because of this, he fell into error. The enemy used error and greed in Balaam's life to destroy his ministry. When truth is on the line, Satan will push us to our breaking point, attempting to infiltrate our lives with error. Your enemy is constantly looking for weak places to attack you in order to circumvent the will of God in your life. If he sees a door open to lead you into error, he will try to use it to destroy you.

Error follows a clear path in your life. If you can learn to recognize and understand that path, you can prevent errors from happening. You cannot keep error from coming and trying to seduce you, but you do not have to fall for it! Balaam's path to error came in through the temptation of money. Your path to error may be something else. The enemy may try to use popularity, fame, and prestige to entice you. He may try to use power or influence. Whatever your weakness is, you must decide that you will not sell out, no matter how high the offer gets.

The first thing about the spirit of error I want you to know is that it always begins with sincerity (Numbers 22:7-11). Many people are sincere, but they are sincerely wrong. Balaam was not looking to fall into a trap. The enticement began with something good: someone called upon him to use the gift that God had entrusted to him. The devil never gives you the full implications of your sin at the outset.

> You cannot keep error from coming and trying to seduce you, but you do not have to fall for it!

When he tempts people with drugs, he doesn't say, "I want you to take something that will make you feel good for a few minutes, but eventually will kill you." He begins with something that will appeal to you.

Ignorance is the absence of truth, and Balaam was not ignorant. This brings me to my second point about error. Balaam knew the truth, and he knew the rules. He knew that the Israelites were God's nation, and that they were a blessed nation. He knew that he would be working against the blessing of God if he tried to curse them. Even though he knew the rules, he attempted to bend or break them. It is a blatant error when you know the rules but decide not to follow them.

Thirdly, error begins to gain a foothold when we question God's Word and doubt His clearly-revealed truths. Have you ever questioned something God said to or about you? For example, look at the story of Adam and Eve. The devil tricked Adam and Eve by bringing error into their life. He caused them to question the truth as revealed by God. "Has God indeed said, 'You shall not eat of every tree of the garden?'" (Genesis 3:1b, NKJV) Satan put the thought in Eve's head to question what God had told her. We read the Bible, know what the Bible says on a certain issue, and still question it. Many of you are at a crossroads in your life. You stand at a place where you must make a decision. You must choose between error and truth. If you willfully choose to make an error, it can lead to your destruction. If you choose the truth, God will begin to turn you around and get you on the right path.

Let me show you another person who chose the path of error. God told King Saul to go and utterly destroy the Amalekites (1 Samuel 15). He instructed Saul to leave nothing standing—to take man, beast, and everything and put it under "the band," which means to utterly destroy and wipe it out. King Saul destroyed the Amalekites as God instructed. He wiped everything out—everything except their king and some choice animals. Saul knew that, in the natural, you never go to war without bringing back some of the spoils. He reasoned that maybe he could bring back the king to show his people that he had whipped the enemy. He did this out of fear of the people (v. 24) and a little pride and selfishness.

So many times in Saul's life, he only partially obeyed God's instructions. If he would have fully obeyed the truths that God made so plain to him, it could have altered the course of his reign. But he insisted on believing only bits and pieces of what God said, deviating to what he wanted when it became more convenient.

Partial obedience is error. The problem with our society is that we only obey what we want to obey. We obey what we like. We obey what is convenient. We do what feels good, creating excuses for why we do not have to do what God said. Because Saul disobeyed God, God chose to rip his kingdom away from him and give it to another. Saul followed the way of error and experienced great loss.

Another person in the Bible who followed the way of error is Gehazi (2 Kings 5), a servant to the prophet Elisha. There was a great warrior in the Syrian army named Naaman who had leprosy. Naaman asked Elisha to pray for God to heal him. When Naaman showed up at Elisha's home, Elisha would not even go out to see him. Instead, he sent his servant Gehazi with a message: "Go and wash in the Jordan seven times . . . and you shall be clean" (2 Kings 5:10, NKJV). Although resistant at first, Naaman washed in the Jordan seven times and was healed.

Naaman was the commander of the Syrian army, a very wealthy man. The king of Syria had given him gifts to take with him for the prophet Elisha, in case he needed to buy a cure. After being healed, Naaman was prepared to reward Elisha generously, but Elisha refused. He had a gift from God that could not be bought. But Gehazi had what he thought was a brilliant idea: "Maybe we will take some of that money. What could it hurt?" He took some of Naaman's money. God revealed to Elisha that Gehazi had fallen into error. He had lied and cheated. Gehazi was stricken with leprosy. His error devastated him.

Let's go back to our study on Balaam and discover the fourth principle on the path of error: error always leads us away from God and our desire for Him. The prophet Balaam, who was once open to God's voice—so much so that God had used him as a mouthpiece—could not even see as far into the spiritual realm as the donkey he was riding. Balaam had become blinded by greed and error. His spiritual eyes had been darkened by

> Error always leads us away from God and our desire for Him.

his disobedience. That leads us to the next principle: how your errors affect others.

Fifth, do not think you can live life in error and not negatively impact others. Do not think that your sin does not violate other people. It may not hurt an entire nation—it may not even affect an entire church—but it will at least affect the people with whom you are living. As much as I love my wife, Robin, I have hurt her. I have said and done things that were not right. I have made decisions in the church that have affected many people. Just as your single act of obedience can become somebody's miracle, your single act of disobedience may inevitably affect others and cause them to fall into sin.

Balaam's error negatively affected an entire nation. After he gave four prophecies, he realized he could not curse Israel because they were a blessed nation. When Balaam realized that he could not succeed with his task, he began to concoct a way to hurt Israel. Balaam told Balak the secret to cursing Israel. He knew that, if he could get them into disobedience, they would begin to lose the blessing. Balak then seduced and deceived the Israelites, leading them into error. Balaam's sin infiltrated a vast majority of the nation. Error is extremely dangerous, because it spreads from one person to another. Be careful that you are not enticed by its deceptiveness.

The sixth factor in the path to error is that error is close enough to the truth to deceive, yet contaminated enough to bring destructive results. If errors were blatant, it would be much more difficult for us to buy into them. God gave Balaam permission to go, but only if they came to call on him again. However, as soon as he was given permission to go, he left without waiting to be asked. God was angry with him for not following His word. Error is often close to the truth. We have learned to use Scripture to justify doing what we want to do instead of what God has said to do. We often fail to obey God because it is too difficult, it costs us too much, or it requires us to do something we do not want to do.

Lastly, error begins when our thinking gets out of line with God's stated will and purpose for our lives. It is imperative that we bring our wrong thinking into captivity, or it will lead us into captivity. Remember the Apostle Paul's directive to the Corinthian Church in 2 Corinthians 10:3-6 (NKJV):

For though we walk in the flesh, we do not war according to the flesh. For the weapons of our warfare are not carnal but mighty in God for pulling down strongholds, casting down arguments and every high thing that exalts itself against the knowledge of God, bringing every thought into captivity to the obedience of Christ, and being ready to punish all disobedience when your obedience is fulfilled.

FROM ERROR TO TRUTH AND OBEDIENCE

There are two ways to combat the spirit of error. The first way to combat it is to know the truth. Many Christians are totally oblivious to the truth. They have no idea what the Bible says! They want to walk free from error but do not put forth any time to read the Word. If you want to walk in the truth, you must spend time reading the Bible. Jesus said, "You shall know the truth, and the truth shall make you free" (John 8:32, NKJV). The prerequisite to the truth setting you free is that you know it. If you do not know the truth, it is not doing you any good. So, get into the Word—whether that's with your print Bible, an app, or listening to the Word in your car. Make time to pour God's truth into your spirit.

The second thing you must do to combat error is to live in obedience to the truth. There are plenty of people who know the truth about Jesus Christ but do not walk in it. The devil knows the truth but is not obedient to it. After you study God's Word, you must internalize it and begin to live it. While some people only have head knowledge of the truth, the knowledge that leads to liberation is the kind that comes from a relationship with Christ. After reading the Word, come into a relationship with the Living Word. Jesus said, "If you love me, keep my commands" (John 14:15, NIV). Let God's Word infiltrate every aspect of your day, from your work to your phone calls to your water cooler talk. Pastors and church leaders, allow God to examine your hearts. Jesus spoke to the messenger of the church of Pergamos in Revelation 2:14 (ESV) and said,

> *"But I have a few things against you: you have some there*
> *who hold the teaching of Balaam, who taught Balak to put a*
> *stumbling block before the sons of Israel, so that they might eat*
> *food sacrificed to idols and practice sexual immorality."*

Jesus told this church to stay away from the error of Balaam. This spirit can be rampant in churches, families, communities, and nations, wreaking havoc wherever it shows its ugly face. Again, Peter writes to the church and says, "They have forsaken the right way and gone astray, following the way of Balaam the son of Beor . . ." (2 Peter 2:15, NKJV). Sadly, pastors are often coming in and preaching the truth, but a spirit of error is hanging over the congregation, so nobody is able to receive and believe the truth. Likewise, business leaders lead their companies astray when they walk in the way of the world instead of by the principles of God's Word. If you know the truth, stand for it, and walk in it, you will not follow the path of error. If you choose to believe God's Word, keep your eyes on Him, and walk in obedience, He will guard your heart from the path of error.

The spirit of error worked in Balaam because he had a propensity toward greed, popularity, power, and fame. I do not know what will bring error out for you, but you need to find out and close those doors. Turn your heart towards God and His truth. Stand on His Word and do what He tells you to do. Understand that you are reliant on Him to help you do what His Word says. Lean into and upon the Lord.

All of us have, at some level, fallen to the power of our flesh and committed error. God has been merciful to you in your error because He is committed to the process of bringing you to the truth. Allow the Holy Spirit to show you the truth. Many are faced with the dilemma of choice. You can choose to walk in the truth or in error. If you choose to walk in the truth, God will empower you to do so. Let me conclude by saying this: many people do not have a problem with what I am saying concerning what they should not do; but it is just as much an error when God reveals a truth to you and you do not walk in it simply because someone might not understand your liberty. The Bible is not just about what we cannot do or cannot have; it is equally emphatic about what we can have and can do.

If you believe that you may be susceptible to the spirit of error, pray this prayer with me:

Dear Father,

I come to You in the Name of Jesus and acknowledge my struggle with error and greed. I have been exposed to the truth in Your Word about how the enemy tries to operate on or through me and I reject and renounce it today in Jesus' Name. Your Word also says that when I know Your truth, "the truth will set you free" (John 8:32, ESV). I receive the truth of Your Word today and declare that, "If the Son sets you free, you will be free indeed" (John 8:36, NIV), and by faith in Your finished work at Calvary, I AM FREE!

I pray now, fill me fresh with Your Spirit and wisdom to walk in this freedom and experience the joy You have designed for my life. Amen!

CHAPTER FOUR

FROM DISLOYALTY TO LOYALTY

After this it happened that Absalom provided himself with chariots and horses, and fifty men to run before him. Now Absalom would rise early and stand beside the way to the gate. So it was, whenever anyone who at a lawsuit came to the king for a decision, that Absalom would call to him and say, "What city are you from?" And he would say, "Your servant is from such and such a tribe of Israel." Then Absalom would say to him, "Look, your case is good and right; but there is no deputy of the king to hear you." Moreover Absalom would say, "Oh, that I were made judge in the land, and everyone who has any suit or cause would come to me; then I would give him justice." And so it was, whenever anyone came near to bow down to him, that he would put out his hand and take him and kiss him. In this manner Absalom acted toward all Israel who came to the king for judgment. So Absalom stole the hearts of the men of Israel.
—2 Samuel 15:1-6 (NKJV)

Something hit the economies of the world in March 2020. That something became known as COVID-19. Although we have moved out of the pandemic phase of the virus, we are still trying to navigate our way to whatever will be our new normal. Nothing was left unaffected by the virus. Individuals, families, churches, businesses, schools, governments—on and on goes the list—were all negatively impacted.

On top of the virus, a social justice crisis brought another layer to our cultural shift. Many individuals adopted new brands that aligned with their values and dropped those that failed to adjust to many customers' expectations. According to a study done by the Omnicom Media Group cited in an article put out by Campaign US in January 19, 2021, almost half (49%) of the people in the study said they switched brands to "take a stand" in response to a brand's behavior amid the social justice crisis of 2020.

As I stated earlier, virtually nothing was left untouched by the effects of the virus and the social justice movement. Churches were impacted in such a big way that many saw a dramatic decline in attendance. Online church became the new norm, and for many it still is.

Loyalties to almost everything were challenged and are still being challenged. It is my humble opinion that disloyalty is happening because we failed to understand the shifts happening in our society as well as in the church. We can no longer ignore the need to rebuild the spirit of loyalty that is so desperately needed in our churches.

The church and church leaders, like companies that are scrambling to regain customer loyalty, must do some real soul-searching to determine what is missing and what is needed by this generation of the unchurched and de-churched. When people lose faith in the church's leaders and institutions, only those leaders and institutions can regain that commitment.

While we are experiencing unprecedented times, the church has been in this predicament before. Even a casual study of church history will reveal that the church has faced many crises before now. The True Leader of the Church, Jesus Christ, guided the church forward then, and will guide us forward again.

WHAT IS DISLOYALTY?

To be disloyal is to fail to honor your duties, obligations, and commitments to others. Disloyalty fails to honor others, and therefore it fails to honor God. Think about how dangerous that is! When we operate in loyalty, we honor God and others. A disloyal person is one who is not trustworthy. Spiritually speaking, we can say that this individual is not committed, lacks consistency, and is not devoted to the cause.

When people's perceptions of the church and its leadership are shaken, we can't get mad and attack them; we must do the hard work of church-evaluation and self-evaluation. Not all disloyalty can or will be turned around—not all loyalty will be regained. The potential is always there, but the process and path to regain loyalty must be followed.

The truth is that most people don't get up one day and decide to be disloyal to whatever institutions hold their loyalties. Something almost always happens to reveal the cracks in our loyalty armor. Just like the worldwide fallout in church attendance we're experiencing didn't happen in a vacuum, neither will the solution simply happen.

In this chapter, we will see a powerful example of our enemy taking advantage of a relational and emotional wound that was left unattended. This wound became the door for offense and disappointment to creep into someone's life. This failure of leadership was used by the devil to produce disloyalty in the heart of one of the sons of King David and the nation of Israel.

THE DISLOYALTY OF ABSALOM

We see disloyalty in King David's son, Absalom. Unfortunately, Absalom failed to honor his father, the king of the nation. This happened at a time when his father needed him the most. In this story, Absalom allowed bitterness and unforgiveness toward his father to grow into a spirit of disloyalty. The spirit of Absalom is the spirit of disloyalty. Disloyalty surfaces when personal ambition and unresolved offense lead to unforgiveness.

In Luke 17:1 (NKJV), Jesus states, "It is impossible that no offenses should come..." If you have never been offended by anyone, either you are perfect or you live on a different planet than I do. I promise you this: you will have plenty of opportunities to get offended with people—in person or online, in church or in business. Whether you allow yourself to become offended is up to you.

THE CAUSES OF DISLOYALTY

Unresolved offense is the first door through which Satan attacks to create a spirit of disloyalty in your life. If you do not watch your attitude towards others, it will be easy to get offended. Someone could say the wrong thing at the wrong time. Someone could not say something when a word needs to be spoken. Someone could look at you the wrong way. Someone could fail to look at you. Someone could tag you in a post. Someone could unfollow you. There are many opportunities in life for offense to come.

When you get offended with people, you begin to think negative thoughts about them. Negative thoughts lead to judgments as well as criticism. Judgments and criticism lead to a spirit of disloyalty. Offense is a sneaky trap in which the devil desires to catch you.

Let me illustrate the trap of offense. The Greek word for offense is *skandalon*, from which we get the English word *scandal*. Skandalon means a "trap stick." As a child, I used to get a box, put a carrot inside, and prop it up with a trap stick. I was trying to catch a rabbit. I would tie a string to the stick and hide behind a bush until the rabbit crawled under the box to get the food and—*yank*—I'd pull the string! That is exactly what offense, or *skandalon*, is. It is a trap the devil wants you to get caught in; and when you get offended with someone and take the bait, it is almost impossible not to have an offense . . .

Nursing an offense will produce the fruit of unforgiveness, a critical and judgmental spirit, an insulting and wounding attitude, divisiveness, backbiting, and of course, betrayal! Yikes! The devil pulls the trap stick. Disloyalty begins to root in your life. You talk negatively about the person. You unfollow them or block them out of spite. You begin to harbor bitterness and malice toward them. Absalom allowed his unresolved offense to become a catalyst. It caused him to work against the man he was supposed to be serving. The Bible says that he stole the hearts of the men of Israel (See 2 Samuel 15:6). His offense caused him to try to bring harm to another human being—even his father. He took over the throne in the wrong way. He ran his father out of the country, threatening his very life.

Since unresolved offense is the first door through which Satan attacks to create a spirit of disloyalty, it becomes important to note two distinct perspectives of offense. First, some people get offended because another person has treated them unjustly. It can be easy to get offended when someone truly wrongs you. I am sure that, in the course of your life, someone has done something extremely cruel to you. It can be hard to forgive another person in that situation. Bitterness can take root in your life if you do not forgive. However, one of the worst outcomes of unforgiveness is realized when you do not even have to be wronged to become offended. Some people have carried so much hurt for so long that they get offended frequently for no reason at all. When we become offended, we often feel that our "rights" have been violated. Learn to forgive, or it will cause you much more pain than it is worth. Jesus said, "And blessed is he who is not offended because of Me" (Luke 7:23, NKJV).

> Learn to forgive, or it will cause you much more pain than it is worth.

The second door through which Satan attacks in an effort to turn you towards disloyalty is selfish ambition. Absalom was carrying an unresolved offense against his father, David, because David didn't deal with Absalom's brother Amnon when Amnon raped their sister Tamar (2 Samuel 13). When you see someone in a place of authority and believe that you are more gifted than they are in certain areas, don't try to show them up. God has put them in that place of leadership as a gift to the body of Christ (1 Corinthians 12:27-28). Serve them and help them. If you serve faithfully, God will bless you for being humble. He may open up another door for you to lead or find creative ways for you to utilize your gifts to serve right where you are.

Another thing you must guard against is trying to control people who are under you and are extremely gifted in certain areas. You can tell this is happening when you will not release these individuals to use their gifts. You want to be the King Daddy. You want the recognition. Your pride gets in the way of allowing kingdom work to be done. I know of pastors who want and need help but are so insecure that they cannot receive it. Pastors who foster the spirit of competition among their staff are setting up themselves, and those serving them, for failure.

For those of you in a staff or support role, learn how to deflect praise. When praise comes to you from someone in the congregation or group, receive the kind words with a "thank you," then pass the praise on to your leader and to God. By doing this, you close the door on suspicion and jealousy.

Both of these scenarios exemplify how ambition can lead to selfishness in your life. Selfish ambition can cause you to stab someone close to you in the back. It can cause you to betray someone you are supposed to be serving. It even can cause you to hurt someone you love or once loved. Absalom betrayed his own father.

OVERCOMING DISLOYALTY WITH LOYALTY

Biblical loyalty is the belonging, commitment, and solidarity with the message and cause of Christ. Loyalty means our whole being is completely and thoroughly devoted to God's way. We see this type of loyalty exemplified in Joshua when he made this powerful declaration in Joshua 24:15 (NKJV): ". . . Choose for yourselves this day whom you will serve . . . But as for me and my house, we will serve the Lord."

Biblical loyalty can only be gained when we are willing to repent of our self-centered and selfish ambitions, which block the flow of the Spirit that is intended to help us maintain a servant's heart. Everyone needs to be a servant to God and to someone else. You cannot accomplish anything in the kingdom of God alone. You need others. I am blessed with a gifted and loyal staff that supports the vision God has given to Seven Springs Church and to me. I believe that this loyalty was established and is maintained because we try to believe the best about each other and to communicate honestly with one another.

Biblical loyalty can't be maintained if you do not talk to one another. If you don't communicate honestly with one another, you cannot keep the door of offense closed. If you are in ministry, you need to pull gifted people close to you to help you, because God did not call you to accomplish your destiny alone. If you are in business, surround yourself with leaders who will pull you closer to the Lord and help you walk in His ways. In the same spirit, do not help others simply because you think you can do a better job than them, or because you know more than they do about a certain situation; but truly serve your leader because it is the right thing to do and because you love and honor them.

> If you don't communicate honestly with one another, you cannot keep the door of offense closed.

Biblical loyalty is greatly enhanced by serving with a humble heart. James 4:10 (NKJV) says, "Humble yourselves in the sight of the Lord, and He will lift you up." You do not need a name badge or a title to accomplish great things for God. People discover what you are able to do because you are serving in your area of giftedness. Then, you must allow God to elevate you. He will. But first, you must be willing to serve somebody.

One of the most difficult things to accomplish as a leader is surrounding yourself with a gifted and loyal team so that you can carry out God's vision for His kingdom work. But if you are going to be successful and happy, you are going to have to learn to do this. It is also just as important that those called to serve a leader learn to let their God-given vision flow through the vision of the person they are called to serve.

Judas fell victim to selfish desires. When the woman broke the alabaster box over the feet of Jesus, Judas took the opportunity to criticize her waste of the expensive perfume (John 12:5). The truth of the matter is that Judas could not stand that Jesus was being celebrated. It is hard to keep our motives and attitudes right if we do not see ourselves as an instrument being used for the good of kingdom work. Judas failed to see his worth to Jesus and the vision that Jesus was sent to accomplish.

Learn to come under the authority of the people God has placed in your life, even if they are not always right. Follow the example of King David, who came under the authority of Saul, even when Saul was trying to kill him (1 Samuel 18:1-9; 19:1-3). Sometimes, you have to come under bad authority. David had the chance to kill Saul (1 Samuel 24 and 26)—and Saul probably deserved death for all the wickedness he had done, but David refused to do this because he understood authority (1 Samuel 26:8-12). God dealt with Saul and blessed David for his obedience. If you are serving a leader who is corrupt, do not take it upon yourself to attempt to destroy that person. Allow God to deal with them. God will bless you for coming under authority.

Are you being controlled by a desire to be recognized and promoted? Are you carrying around unresolved offense against someone who may or may not have truly offended you? Allow God to help you release it right now. Be free from the bondage that Satan has enslaved you to by causing you to believe that you can never forgive. The Old Testament figure of Joseph is the perfect example of how we should respond to offense. Joseph's jealous brothers sold him into slavery because his father showed favoritism toward him. Then, his owner's wife falsely accused Joseph of rape when he refused her sexual advances. He was placed in prison for over twelve years. All the while, Joseph continued to serve with a right attitude. When the opportunity came to use his God-given gift to interpret the dream of Pharaoh, he was elevated to second-in-command of all Egypt (Genesis 37–50). I believe this happened, in part, because Joseph was able to forgive those who had wronged him and to keep serving those over him. I encourage you to read the story of Joseph and notice carefully the evolution of his attitude from a young, overconfident favorite son to a humble servant-leader.

In closing, it is important to note the words of Jesus and how He instructed us to overcome the spirit of offense in Luke 17:1-4 (NKJV):

> . . . *It is impossible that no offenses should come, but woe to him through whom they do come! It would be better for him if a millstone were hung around his neck, and he were thrown into the sea, than that he should offend one of these little ones. Take heed to yourselves. If your brother sins against you, rebuke him; and if he repents, forgive him. And if he sins against you seven times in a day, and seven times in a day returns to you, saying, "I repent," you shall forgive him.*

If you are carrying around offense, pray this prayer with me:

Dear Father,

I come to You in the Name of Jesus and acknowledge my struggle with disloyalty. I have been exposed to the truth in Your Word about how the enemy tries to operate on or through me and I reject and renounce it today in Jesus' Name. Your Word also says that when I know Your truth, "the truth will set you free" (John 8:32, ESV). I receive the truth of Your Word today and declare that, "If the Son sets you free, you will be free indeed" (John 8:36, NIV), and by faith in Your finished work at Calvary, I AM FREE!

I pray now, fill me fresh with Your Spirit and wisdom to walk in this freedom and experience the joy You have designed for my life. Amen!

CHAPTER FIVE

FROM CONTROL TO SERVANTHOOD

*And it came to pass, as though it had been a trivial thing for him
to walk in the sins of Jeroboam the son of Nebat, that he took as
wife Jezebel the daughter of Ethbaal, king of the Sidonians; and he
went and served Baal and worshiped him. Then he set up an altar
for Baal in the temple of Baal, which he had built in Samaria.*
—1 Kings 16:31-32 (NKJV)

*And Ahab told Jezebel all that Elijah had done, also how he had
executed all the prophets with the sword. Then Jezebel sent a messenger
to Elijah, saying, "So let the gods do to me, and more also, if I do not
make your life as the life of one of them by tomorrow about this time."*
—1 Kings 19:1-2 (NKJV)

'm not sure if the accounts are all true or not, but many credible
historians believe that, between October 1919, and March 1921, the

United States was run by a lady named Edith Wilson. Edith, the First Lady and wife of Woodrow Wilson, the 28th President, helped to keep the severe stroke her husband had a secret. She would go into his room to consult him on matters and come out with the decision, but most believe that she was actually making the decisions herself. Edith Wilson did this while her husband was incapacitated. Later in this chapter, we will talk about another first lady who sought to control her husband . . . but this first lady desired to pull a nation away from God.

WHAT IS CONTROL?

Control, in this sense, is an unfair influence over someone. Control seeks to manipulate, intimidate, or dominate someone else. A person operating in the spirit of control is not the leader, but they seek to control the leader through subversive actions. They may do this by trying to manipulate, intimidate, or even blackmail the leader. Earlier in this book, we read about rebellion. Rebellion is usually open and direct. People who rebel want the leader to be replaced, and may actually want to be the leader themselves. Control and manipulation are usually more cunning and indirect. Control can be open and direct, but the person who wants to control doesn't necessarily want to be the leader. Often, they are content to simply dictate the leader's actions.

Manipulators—controlling people—are almost always self-centered. They want what they want, when they want it and how they want it. We've all encountered controlling people—truth be told, most of us have been guilty of controlling others. Of course, when we do it, it is always for the other person's good—at least, that's what we tell ourselves.

THE CONTROL OF JEZEBEL

The spirit of Jezebel is not about a certain gender. It is about trying to control and manipulate people into doing what you want them to do.

It is a spirit of manipulation, control, and intimidation. Jezebel was a tyrant who corrupted her husband, her family, and an entire nation.

The name Jezebel is believed to be of Phoenician origin, and most likely means, *"Baal is exalted."* Jezebel was married to King Ahab, king of Israel (1 Kings 16:31). King Ahab was a weak leader who was easily manipulated and dominated by his new wife. One of Queen Jezebel's first acts was to exterminate all the prophets of the Lord (1 Kings 18:4, 13) and set up altars to her Phoenician god, Baal. She sought to exalt herself to the highest position in Israel, but God did not call her to that. Her influence was so pervasive that our Lord Jesus used her name to reference a woman who led the church in Thyatira into the worship of false gods and into sexual debauchery (Revelation 2:20).

When Jezebel married Ahab, they decided to turn the entire city of Samaria into a center for pagan worship, with the main god being Baal. The wicked queen soon became the power behind the throne, though she was not on it. Her corruption would also negatively influence the reign of her son, Ahaziah, who became king after Ahab's death (1 Kings 22:51).

As we'll explore in a little more detail in this chapter, Jezebel had a staunch enemy by the name of Elijah. This great prophet of God stood squarely against Jezebel's rule. He first declared a drought in Israel that lasted for a full three years (James 5:17). This pronouncement ultimately led Elijah to a showdown on Mount Carmel that pitted the 450 priests of Baal and the 400 priests of Asherah against the God of Israel (1 Kings 18:16-46).

THE EFFECTS OF CONTROL

The spirit of control is ruining many of our churches, destroying marriages, and infiltrating every aspect of our lives; yet often, we do not even recognize it! You may not want to hear it, but leaders must expose the spirit of control in our churches so that we can be free from it. We control one another in three main ways: manipulation, intimidation, and domination.

> We control one another in three main ways: manipulation, intimidation, and domination.

The first tool the enemy wants us to use to control others is manipulation. Manipulation is very covert. It says, "I'll trick you into doing what I want."

Intimidation is both covert and overt. People who intimidate others attempt to scare them into doing what they want them to do. Intimidation relies on fear to operate. The Bible says, ". . . perfect love casts out fear . . ." (1 John 4:18, NKJV).

Domination is more overt. It comes right up to you and says, "I am going to make you do what I want you to do." A dominating person relies on the strength of his physique or his personality to control.

God, who is all-powerful, all-knowing, and ever-present could control through manipulation, domination, and intimidation, yet He chooses to operate by the power of love. Conversely, in our society, we have learned to intimidate, manipulate, and control other people into conforming to our own personal agendas and to call these corrupt behaviors "leadership." In reality, they are not leadership tactics but witchcraft. When I use the word witchcraft, I am not talking about an old, pointy-nosed woman brewing up some alligator tails and holding a broom. I am talking about controlling another person's life. Let us look at how the spirit of control operates in the home and the church.

How does Jezebel operate in your family? Let me give you several examples of how it appears:

We see the spirit of Jezebel in operation when children pitch a fit in order to get what they want.

Have you ever been in a grocery store and seen a child pitch an unholy fit, disrupting the entire store? There is a spirit operating on that child that needs to be broken with the right hand of fellowship. You do not explain it away or negotiate with the child. Instead, you say, "Straighten up!" Some people would call this child abuse, but you cannot play around with the beginning of a stronghold in a child's life.

We witness the spirit of Jezebel in the home when one spouse uses their mood to manipulate the behavior of the rest of the family.

This sounds something like this: "If you keep behaving like that, you are not going to get any!" I am tired of homes being messed up because husbands and wives are manipulating and controlling one another. It is often like a chess game, in which spouses attempt to outmaneuver their loved ones.

We see the spirit of control in action when one parent threatens to take the kids and leave if the other does not change a behavior.

What happens to the children? The children begin to take ownership of the separation, feeling as if they are to blame. Stop using your children as pawns to get your way. Close the door, work it out between the adults, and leave your children out of it.

Older children will often attempt to manipulate parents by threatening to leave home if the rules do not change.

The spirit of Jezebel is in operation, trying to manipulate the parents—who are in rightful authority—into changing the rules. "If you do not let me do what I want, I'll go live on the streets. I'll sell drugs. I'll be a prostitute," the spirit of manipulation says. Your response should be, "I love you, but bye!" You cannot allow a child to use manipulative tactics to affect your authority as a parent. You may have made some mistakes, but you must let your child know that, despite these, you will not be threatened and controlled by them.

We see the spirit of Jezebel in operation when a parent discourages a son or daughter from leaving home when it is well past time for them to do so.

Many children are 21, 22, or 25 years old and still sitting around eating Hostess Ding Dongs and Cheerios. If they are going to stay at home, instill in them a work ethic. Make them get out and mow the lawn. Then, when they find someone they love who loves them back, do not stand in their way. Bless them and release them.

We see the spirit of Jezebel in operation when one spouse dominates the other in order to maintain control.

Men are notorious for this. They believe that, since they are bigger and stronger than their spouses, they can run the show. When they walk in, they expect everybody to jump. Why not try putting your arms around your spouse and loving her? Learn to be strong as steel yet soft as velvet.

We see the spirit of Jezebel in operation when physical or mental abuse is used to control.

There are men and women reading this book right now whose lives have been torn apart by abuse. Men, quit hitting your wives. Ladies, quit hitting your husbands just because you know they will not hit back.

Stop the poor, "pitiful me" mind games. Your pouting and moods are destroying lives all around you. Stop it and grow up!

JEZEBEL IN THE CHURCH

The spirit of Jezebel is not foreign to houses of worship in this country. Jezebel did not want to be the leader; she wanted to control the leader. The spirit of Jezebel is the same in the church and in business: it operates through an individual who wants to get their way by manipulating the pastor or other leaders, using them like puppets on a string.

Jezebel's agenda in the church is simple: false teaching and undermining any spiritual authority that keeps it from doing what it wants, when it wants. When any spiritual authority does something that Jezebel does not want, she will put a stop to it. Men and women who operate under this spirit have no concept of the church being bigger than their own opinions or agendas. They are only concerned about their selfish desires and what they want to see happen in the church. They have no regard for the body of Christ or for the lost outside the church. Jezebel loves to find secrets about the leader so that it can use them to control or manipulate him or her.

Jezebel can try to control and manipulate leaders in the house of God, but this spirit works most effectively against weak leaders. When a leader fails to lead, he or she begins to forfeit their position of leadership. Jezebel often takes advantage of this situation by controlling the leader. Leaders who desire to please people instead of God are especially susceptible to the spirit of Jezebel.

I used to be that kind of pastor. I was controlled by what people thought of me, how people felt about me, and how people responded to me. If you live like that, you have a very tough road ahead of you. There is a good chance you are either going to be unsuccessful or miserable your entire career. I finally reached a point where I made up my mind that God has called me and He is on my side. I cannot control what others think about me, but God loves me.

> Leaders who desire to please people instead of God are especially susceptible to the spirit of Jezebel.

The spirit of Jezebel will go to ridiculous extremes to control a leader. I look out upon many faces every Sunday. I watch people's body language. People will try to control the flow of the service by projecting a certain type of body language. I told my music minister, "Forget people's faces. Sing to God. Let Him direct the flow of the service, not people!" Worship directors, pastors, and leaders, you had better get past the look on people's faces and get after God. If you judge the flow of God by the congregation's body language, you will severely hinder what God wants to do. "I don't like this song. I'm going to sit down," says the church member. Manipulation! If you are attending a church where you sit out in the congregation every Sunday, get behind your choir. Get up on your feet. Get behind your worship leader. Get in there with your pastor and help him preach! Do not try to manipulate a move of God. Just go where your leader is trying to take you as he or she follows after the Lord.

The same is true in business: if you encounter those who are trying to derail and manipulate people away from the agenda that the Lord has laid out before your leader, support your leader and do what you can do to discourage this attempt at control.

FROM CONTROL TO SERVANTHOOD

When attempting to stop the spirit of Jezebel, the temptation is to try to fight fire with fire. You cannot come against control and manipulation using control and manipulation. You must come against Jezebel with godly authority. You must surrender your will and your desires, allowing His purpose to take over. Then you can fully submit to His purpose in your life. You cannot be timid in dealing with this spirit. You must resist it by standing firmly on the principles of God's Word and not waffling and wavering. We must remember: we are not battling a person, but the satanic spirit operating through that individual. The apostle Paul declared,

"For we do not wrestle against flesh and blood, but against principalities, against powers, against the rulers of the darkness of this age, against spiritual hosts of wickedness in the heavenly places."
—Ephesians 6:12, NKJV

I have noticed that the most powerful attitude to exemplify when exposing and dealing with the spirit of Jezebel is the characteristic of godly servanthood. Too often, when we think of servanthood, we think of someone who is submissive to the point of appearing weak. Biblical servanthood is anything but that. To be a servant of God is to be submitted to Him, but never to be a doormat of weakness that others walk on and abuse. One of the most powerful examples of this servant-leadership was Moses. We see in Numbers 12:3 (NKJV) that "... Moses was very humble [interpreted *"meek"* in the KJV], more than all men who were on the face of the earth."

I make the comparison between humility and meekness because to be humble is to understand you are submitted to a power greater than yourself, and to be meek is to have power delegated to you under control. Moses was a great and powerful leader, but he understood that his power came from God. We have that same power available to us through the indwelling of the Holy Spirit (Acts 1:8), but we must access it daily, and always with the intention of demonstrating His power for the good of others.

Now that you understand more about the spirit of Jezebel, do not walk around telling people that they have the spirit of Jezebel on them. Do not judge others according to the word that God has given to you. Examine your own life and let God show you any control, intimidation, or manipulation tactics in your life. After that, if you believe that you see a hindering spirit in the life of another, pray for that person. Pray that God would reveal it to them. If it is a son or daughter, or someone under your authority, find a way to lovingly help that person. But do not use this word to become critical towards others. That is not the way of a servant of God.

If you have attempted to wrongfully control the lives of others, pray this prayer with me:

Dear Father,

I come to You in the Name of Jesus and acknowledge my struggle with control and manipulation. I have been exposed to the truth in Your Word about how the enemy tries to operate on or through me and I reject and renounce it today in Jesus' Name. Your Word also says that when I know Your truth, "the truth will set you free" (John 8:32, ESV). I receive the truth of Your Word today and declare that, "If the Son sets you free, you will be free indeed" (John 8:36, NIV), and by faith in Your finished work at Calvary, I AM FREE!

I pray now, fill me fresh with Your Spirit and wisdom to walk in this freedom and experience the joy You have designed for my life. Amen!

CHAPTER SIX

FROM CONFUSION TO CLARITY

Can you draw out Leviathan with a hook, or snare his tongue with a line which you lower? Can you put a reed through his nose, or pierce his jaw with a hook? Will he make many supplications to you? Will he speak softly to you? Will he make a covenant with you? Will you take him as a servant forever? Will you play with him as with a bird, or will you leash him for your maidens? Will your companions make a banquet of him? Will they apportion him among the merchants? Can you fill his skin with harpoons, or his head with fishing spears? Lay your hand on him; remember the battle—Never do it again!
—Job 41:1-8 (NKJV)

In that day the Lord with His severe sword, great and strong, will punish Leviathan the fleeing serpent, Leviathan that twisted serpent; and He will slay the reptile that is in the sea.
—Isaiah 27:1 (NKJV)

The senior pastor receives a phone call at 1:00 a.m.: "Pastor, please help me! My son is in jail!" The pastor staggers out of bed, throws on the first thing he can find, and makes his way down to the local jail. After two hours of red tape, the pastor pays the bond and the young man is free.

About the same time, one of the church members is just finishing up the night shift. He gets in his car and his nightly drive home takes him past the local jail. Out of the corner of his eye, he sees what looks like . . . "No, it could not be true . . . yes, it's the pastor!" He rushes home. "Honey, wake up! You will never believe what just happened. I was coming home from work and I passed the jail, and guess who I saw? Pastor! His hair was all messed up. His clothes were unkempt. He had spent half the night in jail. What do we do, honey?"

The wife has a brilliant idea: "We must call the elders. Pastor needs prayer." When the pastor gets home, there are five messages on the answering machine. "Pastor, it is Elder Smith. We heard that you spent the night in jail. We heard that you finally came staggering out, drunk as a coot." Notice how much the story changes over time.

CONFUSION: THE TWISTED SERPENT

Confusion is a lack of clarity. The enemy is constantly seeking to twist and pervert God's Word, turning people against God and against one another.

Mentioned in the book of Job, Leviathan was an ancient, massive sea creature. I know what some readers may be thinking: "Why are we talking about not being like a sea creature?" It is because, in the Bible, Leviathan represents so much more. Isaiah 27:1 (NKJV) says,

"In that day the Lord with His severe sword, great and strong,
will punish Leviathan the fleeing serpent, Leviathan that twisted
serpent; and He will slay the reptile that is in the sea."

Leviathan is the twisted serpent, the devil. The spirit of Leviathan is the spirit of confusion. Satan has always been a liar. He is the father of all lies. He wants to take the truth of our words and actions and twist it to bring confusion into the body of Christ. If you try to come against Leviathan in the power of your own flesh, he will destroy you. However, if you come against the twisted serpent with the power of the Spirit, you will overcome it.

Before we examine the causes of Leviathan and how to deal with this spirit, you must understand that he is a very formidable foe. Job 41:9 (NKJV) states, "Indeed, any hope of overcoming him is false; shall one not be overwhelmed at the sight of him?" To try to tackle the spirit of Leviathan in the power of your flesh would be insane. Even on your best day, you are still no match for Satan on his worst day. History is littered with men and women who tried to come against Leviathan in the power of their own flesh. If you believe that you can memorize a series of steps, a formula, or simply throw some Bible verses at him, you have no idea what you are up against.

For so long, we have come at Satan with formulas, objects, and religious rituals. Satan is not afraid of these things. In fact, he loves them, because so many people hide behind their religion. In Ephesians 6:12 (NIV), Paul says:

"For our struggle is not against flesh and blood, but against the
rulers, against the authorities, against the powers of this dark world
and against the spiritual forces of evil in the heavenly realms."

Again, in 2 Corinthians 10:3-4 (NIV), Paul states:

"For though we live in the world, we do not wage war as the world does. The weapons we fight with are not the weapons of the world. On the contrary, they have divine power to demolish strongholds."

Before you tackle the twisted serpent Leviathan, you must be armed with the Spirit and His Word. Leviathan recognizes only those who operate in the authority of Jesus and His blood.

Have you ever found yourself in a situation like the pastor in the story I shared? Something you said, did or posted got distorted . . . or maybe someone told you something and you allowed the enemy to twist it in your mind until it was no longer the truth. In the story I shared, the man reported what he saw, but he added his interpretation, assuming the pastor was in jail for something he'd done and that he'd spent the night getting intoxicated and becoming a nuisance. Satan twisted the man's account. Then, the man told his wife and called the elders before coming to the pastor and giving him the opportunity to explain what had really happened.

> Satan wants to bring confusion into your life.

That is the spirit of Leviathan, or confusion, being manifested. Satan wants to bring confusion into your life. The Bible says that God is not the author of confusion (1 Corinthians 14:33). Confusion comes into your life, family, business, or ministry through two doors: pride and rejection.

The initial way that the spirit of confusion enters into your life is through pride. When Leviathan is operating through you, you think you are the only one that sees, knows, discerns, or understands a matter. Satan tricks you into believing that you are more spiritual than you really are. The moment the twisted serpent tricks you into believing that you have everything worked out, you will fall. Pride always comes before the fall.

The second door Leviathan comes in through is rejection. We frequently see the spirit of rejection in operation in the lives of church people—people with the spirit of rejection walk into a room with the assumption that nobody likes them, wants to talk to them, or wants to be around them. And right behind them, that twisted serpent Leviathan is laughing his eyeballs out, because he has them in a mindset of confusion.

People are rejected for many reasons. Many are rejected because of their outward appearance. They either are too unattractive or too attractive, too black or too white, too short or too tall, too fat or too skinny. This is a painful way for a person to live, always feeling like they do not measure up. No matter what they do, it never seems to be enough. No wonder they are open to this ugly spirit! People experience rejection in their lives for many reasons, but until they come to terms with who they are in Jesus Christ, the spirit of rejection will linger over them.

THE EFFECTS OF CONFUSION

We see the effects of confusion in the story of the Tower of Babel (See Genesis 11:1-9). In this case, God intentionally allowed confusion to set in to frustrate the plans of the people. He did this because their goals were misguided. Their stated goal was to make a name for themselves. As followers of Christ, our goal should not be to make a name for ourselves, but to make His Name known. Yet God stated that, if the people worked in unity towards a common goal, nothing would be impossible for them. Think about how powerful a statement that is.

Because of their misguided goals, God sent a spirit of confusion. The word *"babel"* actually means confusion. Due to this confusion, they were not able to understand one another, and their misguided dream of a huge tower reaching into the sky had to be abandoned. When there is a spirit of confusion present in a church, everything becomes much more challenging. It is difficult to grow. It is difficult to get momentum. The vision is not clear and communication breaks down. You will feel like you're spinning your wheels.

Yet when there is clarity, nothing you set out to achieve will be impossible. Of course, your motives must be godly, or else—just like this story—your efforts will be frustrated. A clear vision coupled with clear communication will almost always reap positive results!

FROM CONFUSION TO CLARITY

Moving from confusion to clarity is a noble goal to which every believer should aspire. Our society is bombarded with what has become known as "fake news." The need for clarity has never been greater, and the time for it is definitely now! Gaining clarity is not a once-and-for-all endeavor, but rather a commitment to maintain in daily spiritual and relational life. Remember this about yourself and others: "I may not be able to do anything about what goes on around me, but I and I alone am responsible for what goes on in me." The following steps may seem rather simple on the surface, but they must be practiced daily and routinely if you want to live consistently free from the twisting of our enemy, Leviathan.

First, do not try to reason with the spirit of Leviathan. Remember, it is going to twist everything you say. If this spirit is influencing your life, everything you hear will be confused. Resist the devil. Keep resisting him. Until, as Isaiah says, God puts the sword to Leviathan and kills the sucker, we must resist him. Believe me, that twisted serpent will get back up and come at you again. Reject him, resist him, and make him flee from your life.

Secondly, remember that only God can really stop Leviathan—therefore, trust God! The more you try to reason with someone operating under the influence of the Leviathan spirit, the more this enemy will use your words. Let your "yes" be yes and your "no" be no. Thank God for putting His sword to the lie by revealing the truth. This is the work of the Holy Spirit, and our part in this step to freedom and victory is to speak clearly and to not use an abundance of words.

Thirdly, stay away from people who cause division. The devil wants to bring confusion into the body of Christ to divide us. If you see a person surrounded by confusion, and arguments seem to always follow them around, there is a strong likelihood that there is a demonic spirit hanging around them. Do not judge them or write them off. Simply pray for them. Paul tells us in Romans 16:17 (NKJV), "... Note [mark] those who cause divisions and offenses, contrary to the doctrine which you learned, and avoid them." When it is necessary to have interaction with these individuals, keep your conversation short and your words concise.

Lastly, when we see that the spirit of confusion is operating or trying to operate in our lives, we must act quickly and, if necessary, repent immediately. Then,

> When we see that the spirit of confusion is operating or trying to operate in our lives, we must act quickly and, if necessary, repent immediately.

purposely begin to speak only the truth. Resist talking all the time. The truth is that we who communicate as part of our work are more susceptible to this spirit trying to operate through us than we might have imagined. This is why the writer of Proverbs gives us clear instruction about the necessity of watching what we say: "You are snared by the words of your mouth; you are taken by the words of your mouth" (Proverbs 6:2, NKJV).

This is also why the Psalmist prayed, "I said, 'I will watch my ways and keep my tongue from sin; I will put a muzzle on my mouth while in the presence of the wicked" (Psalm 39:1, NIV).

Additionally, take a look at his prayer in Psalm 141:1-3 (NKJV):

> *Lord, I cry out to You; make haste to me! Give ear to my voice*
> *when I cry out to You. Let my prayer be set before You as incense,*
> *the lifting up of my hands as the evening sacrifice. Set a guard,*
> *O Lord, over my mouth; keep watch over the door of my lips.*

As leaders, we must set the standard of clear and godly communication! Where possible, exercise control over what you choose to listen to and repeat. Take responsibility for your words and close the door on Leviathan!

Confusion has caused pain in the lives of many people. It comes between spouses, parents and their children, and siblings. Confusion attempts to divide families, churches, and businesses. If you believe that you are dealing with a spirit of confusion in your life, pray this prayer with me:

> *Dear Father,*
>
> *I come to You in the Name of Jesus and acknowledge my struggle*
> *with confusion. I have been exposed to the truth in Your Word*

about how the enemy tries to operate on or through me and I reject and renounce it today in Jesus' Name. Your Word also says that when I know Your truth, "the truth will set you free" (John 8:32, ESV). I receive the truth of Your Word today and declare that, "If the Son sets you free, you will be free indeed" (John 8:36, NIV), and by faith in Your finished work at Calvary, I AM FREE!

I pray now, fill me fresh with Your Spirit and wisdom to walk in this freedom and experience the joy You have designed for my life. Amen!

CHAPTER SEVEN

FROM LEGALISM TO FREEDOM

*"The scribes and the Pharisees sit in Moses' seat. Therefore
whatever they tell you to observe, that observe and do, but do not
do according to their works; for they say, and do not do. . . . But
woe to you, scribes and Pharisees, hypocrites! For you shut up the
kingdom of heaven against men; for you neither go in yourselves,
nor do you allow those who are entering to go in. . . . Serpents,
brood of vipers! How can you escape the condemnation of hell?"*
—Matthew 23:2-3, 13, 33 (NKJV)

I once pastored a man whom I loved and respected very much. This
man would not chew gum. Those of you who know me know I love
chewing gum. My wife gets uncomfortable when I chew gum because
I pop it too much. You will know when I have gum. You will hear me
miles away. I like to have fun with my gum and I want everybody to
enjoy it with me. I know this sounds crazy, but this brother had a

conviction against gum. Do you know why? Because he had a tobacco problem, and if he ever chewed gum, it created the sensation and urge in his mind to chew tobacco. The Lord set him free from tobacco, but in order to walk in obedience to that freedom, he had to give up chewing gum as well.

That was his own personal conviction, and that was fine, because it helped him live out his freedom. But could you imagine him trying to put that conviction onto someone else? This is the problem with legalism: we try to take what has worked for us and make it a law about how things must be done. We expect others to do what we do, the way we do it.

Legalism is not a new phenomenon, but rather has been experienced by other religions and cultures in every time period. What often is intended for good can easily become control.

WHAT IS LEGALISM?

Legalism is excessive adherence to a law or formula. Legalistic behaviors may appear religious, but they actually hinder people from being truly devoted to God with an overemphasis on rules and details.

The story above illustrates one way in which legalism begins. Someone starts with a personal conviction that is not found in God's Word, walks and lives in it, and then tries to enforce it in the life of another believer. How many commandments did God give us? Only ten! In fact, Jesus summed those up in only two commandments in Matthew 22:37-40 (NKJV):

> Jesus said to him, "'You shall love the Lord your God with all your heart, with all your soul, and with all your mind.' This is the first and great commandment. And the second is like it: 'You shall love your neighbor as yourself.' On these two commandments hang all the Law and the Prophets."

If we really believed what Jesus said and practiced it, can you imagine what this world would look like—how exciting it would be? Think about it: Jesus was actually telling us that this is the way to true freedom.

THE LEGALISM OF THE PHARISEES

But the Pharisees did not believe ten was enough, much less the two that Jesus summed everything into in His ministry. They felt they had to assist God by creating more. The Pharisees took God's ten rules and made them into over 600 rules. What that says to me is, "God gave us ten, but that was not sufficient. We want to help You, God, do a better job of making rules. So, we are going to make up some rules of our own and live by them in Your Name."

The Pharisees made up ridiculous rules. God's commandments say that it is unlawful to work on the Sabbath. Since they wanted to make sure no one worked on the Sabbath, the Pharisees made a regulation that people could not spit on the Sabbath, because your spittle would make a furrow—and that is considered plowing. I know of some preachers who would be in big trouble with this rule because, when they preach every Sunday, they spray spittle everywhere. Granted, this may sound absurd, but you get the picture: the Pharisees took things to such extremes that it became ridiculous.

This spirit doesn't just operate in the church, but can and does manifest in our homes, on our jobs, in our schools, and even in our communities. The more rules and regulations you have, the more rules and regulations you need to clarify. Please understand that this spirit will always have control over you . . . it will make life so restrictive that you experience a loss of joy and freedom.

The Pharisaical spirit is perhaps the cruelest of all the spirits that hinders God's anointing because it projects itself as being righteous, holy, and spiritual. This is the spirit that sits in the church with the appearance of having everything together, when in actuality it has a darkened, hard heart. The spirit of the Pharisee is sometimes difficult to notice because it is cloaked in many ways—ways that almost always appear hyper-religious. Sadly, this spirit operates in people who are truly men and women of God but have crossed the line and find themselves trying to be God to someone else. The legalist can't see this spirit operating in their life.

Embodied in this one spirit, you'll find all the other six in some form:

- → Criticism—the Pharisees assassinated Jesus' character.
- → Rebellion—the Pharisees knew the Word of God, yet didn't know the Lord of the Word and rejected Him.
- → Error—the Pharisees resisted the truth of God in Christ because they were greedy for position, power, and recognition.
- → Disloyalty—the Pharisees undermined the authority of Jesus because they wanted it for themselves.
- → Control—the Pharisees were masters of manipulation, intimidation, and domination for the selfish purpose of attaining their own position, power, and recognition.
- → Confusion—the Pharisees were pros at twisting everything Jesus said and did. They had to appear spiritual in order to stay in control.

THE EFFECTS OF LEGALISM

You can always tell when you get around a Pharisee because they have no joy. Someone stole his or her happiness. The Pharisaical spirit despises a liberated, joyful, peaceful, grace-giving believer. This spirit hates to see you happy. It is the same spirit that killed Abel, crucified Christ, stoned Stephen, and imprisoned Paul. It is the same spirit that is trying to knock you and me off our walk with Jesus today. It seeks to blind us by causing us to believe that following rules is a means to a relationship with Christ.

How many churches or companies have ridiculous rules and rituals that cannot be found in the Scriptures? Yet we impose them on people, making these rules a test of membership or fellowship in the body of Christ. The truth is that many of these rules were made up by grandma and grandpa. Just because grandma and grandpa lived by them doesn't make them scriptural. In fact, many of these rules were good for grandma and grandpa in their day and time, but we have made golden calves out of them. Golden calves are traditions that we hold to without even knowing the reason for their existence. We do not dare to change them or revise them. You cannot change some things because people have made them an idol, even though they have no biblical basis.

I want to illustrate seven warning signs to watch for that will help you identify the spirit of the Pharisee.

Pharisees love the praises of men. People like it when others talk positively about them. Almost nobody likes it when people bad-mouth them. But when you reach a place in life where you are motivated fundamentally by what people think about you, you are in big trouble.

Pharisees love positions, titles, and recognition. They do not want the position for the work, but for the title. Pharisees dominate people with traditions, rules, and rituals. They are legalistic and judgmental. They project themselves as super-spiritual and yet refuse correction. They love correcting others, but when the time comes for them to receive correction, they do not want to hear it.

Pharisees despise authority and true biblical leadership. The Pharisee seeks the "chief seat" (Matthew 23:6). They esteem the written Word above the Living Word.

Pharisees worship the Book of the Lord instead of the Lord of the Book. Doctrine should enable us to determine the will of God so that we can obey Him. It should lead us to Christ-likeness. Doctrines of men, conversely, are centered on control, measurement, and restriction. The Pharisee cannot stand to see people living in freedom and enjoying their lives in Christ. Nor can they stand that faith in Jesus and His finished work sets people free without a bunch of binding and loosening of evil spirits in their lives. The Pharisee can quote much Scripture, yet they don't know that Truth is a Person! The Pharisee has made an idol out of the Bible.

> The Pharisee cannot stand to see people living in freedom and enjoying their lives in Christ.

In Matthew 23, Jesus pronounces woe after woe upon the Pharisees. If you feel that this spirit may control or operate through you, you should take heed to these woes:

Pharisees reject the truth and rob others of the truth. Verse 13 (NKJV) says, "But woe to you, scribes and Pharisees, hypocrites! For you shut up the kingdom of heaven against men; for you neither go in yourselves, nor do you allow those who are entering to go in."

Pharisees profess righteousness, but their conduct is unjust. Verse 14 (NKJV) says, "Woe to you, scribes and Pharisees, hypocrites! For you devour widows' houses, and for a pretense make long prayers. Therefore you will receive a greater condemnation."

Pharisees are zealous to win people over to their opinions, not to God. Verse 15 (NKJV) reads, "Woe to you, scribes and Pharisees, hypocrites! For you travel land and sea to win one proselyte, and when he is won, you make him twice as much a son of hell as yourselves."

Pharisees claim to be the only guides in religion, but they are blind to the truth. They have developed their own system of righteousness that does not match the Word of God. Verse 16-17a (NKJV) says, "Woe to you, blind guides, who say, 'Whoever swears by the temple, it is nothing; but whoever swears by the gold of the temple, he is obliged to perform it.' Fools and blind!"

Pharisees have lost all sense of proportion regarding true righteousness, as seen in these words of Jesus in verses 23-24 (NKJV), "Woe to you, scribes and Pharisees, hypocrites! For you pay tithe of mint and anise and cumin, and have neglected the weightier matters of the law: justice and mercy and faith. These you ought to have done, without leaving the others undone. Blind guides, who strain out a gnat and swallow a camel!"

Pharisees pay detailed attention to matters pertaining to ceremonial cleansing of the outer man while blatantly ignoring inner holiness. Verses 25-26 (NKJV) say, "Woe to you, scribes and Pharisees, hypocrites! For you cleanse the outside of the cup and dish, but inside they are full of extortion and self-indulgence. Blind Pharisee, first cleanse the inside of the cup and dish, that the outside of them may be clean also."

Pharisees appear to be righteous on the outside, but inwardly they are morally defiled. Verses 27-28 (NKJV) read, "Woe to you, scribes and Pharisees, hypocrites! For you are like whitewashed tombs which indeed appear beautiful outwardly, but inside are full of dead men's bones and all uncleanness. Even so you also outwardly appear righteous to men, but inside you are full of hypocrisy and lawlessness."

Pharisees claim to be greater than their forefathers in righteousness, but their spirit is the spirit that murdered the Son of God. Verses 29-30 (NKJV) say, "Woe to you, scribes and Pharisees, hypocrites! Because you build the tombs of the prophets and adorn the monuments of the righteous, and say, 'If we had lived in the days of our fathers, we would not have been partakers with them in the blood of the prophets.'"

FROM LEGALISM TO FREEDOM

Jesus reveals the way to combat the spirit of Pharisee when He instructs us in Matthew 23:11-12 (NKJV), "But he who is greatest among you shall be your servant. And whoever exalts himself will be humbled, and he who humbles himself will be exalted." Servanthood and humility. These two simple characteristics are all that Jesus said that was needed to combat this evil spirit of the Pharisee.

> Servanthood and humility. These two simple characteristics are all that Jesus said that was needed to combat this evil spirit of the Pharisee.

Another important thing that enables us to walk in freedom is learning to distinguish man-made traditions from God's timeless principles. As stated earlier, the Pharisees elevated man-made rules to the point where they were even, at times, more important than God's laws.

Most church leaders, who have many years of experience, probably know of a church that nearly split over petty things such as a certain musical instrument on stage. There is no Scripture that says you must have a piano, organ, or any other instrument on stage. There are a lot of golden calves that we hang on to in the church world. When we refuse to let things like these go, we are operating in legalism. When we rely on the Law of the Spirit and seek to please God, we can let go of man-made traditions.

If this critical, judgmental, false religious spirit has overtaken you, pray this prayer with me:

Dear Father,

I come to You in the Name of Jesus and acknowledge my struggle with legalism. I have been exposed to the truth in Your Word about how the enemy tries to operate on or through me and I reject and renounce it today in Jesus' Name. Your Word also says that when I know Your truth, "the truth will set you free" (John 8:32, ESV). I receive the truth of Your Word today and declare that, "If the Son sets you free, you will be free indeed" (John 8:36, NIV), and by faith in Your finished work at Calvary, I AM FREE!

I pray now, fill me fresh with Your Spirit and wisdom to walk in this freedom and experience the joy You have designed for my life. Amen!

CHAPTER EIGHT

FREEDOM THAT PRODUCES THE BLESSINGS AND FLOW OF GOD

Now that we have exposed at least seven spirits that can hinder the flow and presence of God in our lives, our families, our churches, our communities, our businesses, and in the world where we all live, work, and play, the obvious question that must be answered is, "Now what?"

For me, it all comes down to receiving and living in freedom! The Holy Spirit hasn't freed us to merely live our lives thinking only of ourselves. We must never forget that freedom comes with responsibilities.

On June 19, 1963, the president sent a comprehensive civil rights bill to the U.S. Congress. The now-famous March on Washington for jobs and freedom on August 28, 1963, roused the American consciousness on equality when Dr. Martin Luther King Jr. gave his great speech, "I Have a Dream." Afterwards, on July 2, 1964, the Civil Rights Act was signed into law by President Lyndon B. Johnson. This act prohibited discrimination in public places, opened the door for the integration of public schools, and made employment discrimination illegal.

The Civil Rights Act of 1964 was now the law of the land, but it still had to be enacted and walked out by the citizens of the United States. Immediately, new civil rights were made available to all the citizens of our nation, regardless of gender, color, or age; but the process of that act of freedom still had to be walked out by the people.

I used the word *process* intentionally. Just like our nation is still in the *process* of forming a more perfect union, we who have been freed from the work of the enemy—who was controlling so much of our lives—are in the *process* of walking out, or forming, this new-found freedom. We are free, but that freedom must be walked out daily.

UNDERSTANDING THE PROCESS

God wants to make our hearts glad by living in the midst of our lives. The Bible tells us that His blessings flow like a river that is too wide to cross and too deep to wade through. If we surrender to the current of this spiritual river without hindering its flow, we will be refreshed and strengthened for the challenges that lie before us. The psalmist wrote about this river that flows from the throne of God:

God is our refuge and strength, a very present help in trouble. Therefore we will not fear, even though the earth be removed, and though the mountains be carried into the midst of the sea; though its waters roar and be troubled, though the mountains shake with its swelling. There is a river whose streams shall make glad the city of God, the holy place of

the tabernacle of the Most High. God is in the midst of her, she shall not
be moved. God shall help her, just at the break of dawn.
— Psalm 46:1-5 (NKJV)

In the above verses, the psalmist speaks of other waters besides the river of God. These rivers are called (1) waters that roar, (2) waters that are troubled, and (3) waters that are difficult. These troubled waters are like the difficulties we face in life. But God's Word tells us not to worry, because even though there are troubles in our lives, there is a river flowing through it that will make us glad. Those other waters will not overflow to disturb us, distress us, or destroy us, if we continue to trust in Him.

At the time of this writing, people throughout the world are facing one potential crisis after another. World powers seem to be positioning themselves for the possibility of World War III. U.S. citizens, as well as citizens of the world, are facing unprecedented threats at home. Terrorists, armed with biological, chemical, and nuclear weapons, are threatening to enact "holy war" on all those who do not share their viewpoints and agendas. Stock markets are plummeting, gas prices are soaring, unemployment is increasing, and a

> No matter the trials we may face, God's answer is the same: there is a river flowing from His throne to His people; and wherever His river goes, everything its waters touch is set free and infused with life.

barrage of extenuating circumstances are continuing to provoke worry in the minds of people everywhere.

But all these problems are just part of those other waters the psalmist mentioned. No matter the trials we may face, God's answer is the same: there is a river flowing from His throne to His people; and wherever His river goes, everything its waters touch is set free and infused with life. Those who believe in Jesus Christ as Lord of their lives are now embracing a wonderful sense of security and joy because there is a river flowing into their lives—one that makes their hearts glad.

ANCIENT VISION STILL SPEAKING TO US TODAY

The prophet Ezekiel saw a vision of this river of God flowing from God's temple (Ezekiel 47:1-12). A man—actually an angel of the Lord—was guiding Ezekiel in his river vision and told him to go out 1,000 cubits, or about 1,500 feet. The river came up to his ankles, then to his knees, and then to his waist. Finally, it was so deep that it could not be crossed. The different depths of the river represent the varying levels in which we can submit ourselves to the anointing of God. We can be ankle-deep, knee-deep, or waist-deep in a relationship with God . . . or we can be totally immersed in His presence.

When we are ankle-, knee-, or waist-deep, we still have both feet on the ground and can wade back to shore whenever we want to; but once we are in the main current, the flow of the river, we are in over our heads and must completely surrender control. As long as we are in control, we are limited by our ability and insights; but when we move into the waters too deeply to do anything but flow, the Holy Spirit is in full control. This picture is important because it speaks of our relationship with the Holy Spirit. How much of Him do you want?

How desperate are you for the full flow of His presence? That place of complete surrender is where God's abundant blessings are experienced at their greatest potential.

The water flowed toward the eastern region and entered the Dead Sea, and once there, the salty, putrid water became fresh. Wherever the river flowed, everything along it lived. Fruit trees of all kinds grew on both banks of the river, as stated in Ezekiel 47:7-12 (NKJV):

When I returned, there, along the bank of the river, were very many trees on one side and the other. Then he said to me: "This water flows toward the eastern region, goes down into the valley, and enters the sea. When it reaches the sea, its waters are healed. And it shall be that every living thing that moves, wherever the rivers go, will live. There will be a very great multitude of fish, because these waters go there; for they will be healed, and everything will live wherever the river goes. It shall be that fishermen will stand by it from En Gedi to En Eglaim; they will be places for spreading their nets. Their fish will be of the same kinds as the fish of the Great Sea, exceedingly many. But its swamps and marshes will not be healed; they will be given over to salt. Along the bank of the river, on this side and that, will grow all kinds of trees used for food; their leaves will not wither, and their fruit will not fail. They will bear fruit every month, because their water flows from the sanctuary. Their fruit will be for food, and their leaves for medicine."

This life, healing, and fruitfulness is what the hindering spirits we've discussed in this book want to interfere with in your life. Your enemy doesn't want you to be filled with the life and power of the Holy Spirit and go on to be a life-giving instrument of God.

Although this river of life is prophesied to one day appear in Jerusalem (Zechariah 14:8), it symbolizes the power of the Holy Spirit that is now available to us, as well. Knowing that God has power to save and bless us abundantly, we can decide not to let sadness or sorrow control us again. We can refuse to give ourselves to worry or fear. We can surrender to the river, the source of abundant life, and let the Holy Spirit carry us to God's promised place of blessings. We can allow the river of life flowing out of us to keep us secure and happy no matter what is happening in the world around us. The psalmist sang of God's promise to preserve us, and of His river of pleasures from which we are invited to drink:

> *Your mercy, O LORD, is in the heavens; Your faithfulness reaches to the clouds. Your righteousness is like the great mountains; Your judgments are a great deep; O LORD, You preserve man and beast. How precious is Your lovingkindness, O God! Therefore the children of men put their trust under the shadow of Your wings. They are abundantly satisfied with the fullness of Your house, and You give them drink from the river of Your pleasures. For with You is the fountain of life; in Your light we see light.*
> —Psalm 36:5-9 (NKJV)

There is no need for us to be worried, fearful, or overly concerned about world events. We don't have to speculate, ponder, or question what will happen to us. God's river of life and gladness is sure to carry us into a safe place.

THE RIVER OF LIFE IS THE HOLY SPIRIT

Jesus also talked about rivers of living water that flow within His believers:

> *He who believes in Me [who adheres to, trusts in, and relies on Me], as the Scripture has said, "From his innermost being will flow continually rivers of living water." But He was speaking of the [Holy] Spirit, whom those who believed in Him [as Savior]*

were to receive afterward. The Spirit had not yet been given,
because Jesus was not yet glorified (raised to honor).
—John 7:38-39 (AMP)

In Jesus' conversation with the woman at the well, He spoke again of
the source of living water, saying,

But whoever drinks the water that I give him will never be
thirsty again. But the water that I give him will become in
him a spring of water [satisfying his thirst for God] welling up
[continually flowing, bubbling within him] to eternal life.
—John 4:14 (AMP)

Believers in Jesus Christ—those who have received the indwelling
presence of the Holy Spirit—are God's "river people." The Holy Spirit
lives in them as their source of strength, continually filling them with
encouragement and life. Even when unbelievers cannot see any reason
to rejoice, Spirit-filled Christians can enjoy a sense of peace and joy.
This joy is a supernatural gift from God, resulting from the indwelling
presence of the Holy Spirit.

When we believers assemble to study the Word and to worship God,
we leave feeling less burdened than when we arrived. We are renewed,
refreshed, and empowered because, through worship, we have stepped
deeper into God's ever-flowing river of blessings. His Word explains
that this river of life is the Holy Spirit, and that He is available to anyone
who confesses Jesus Christ as Lord.

The Holy Spirit is given to us as a seal of promise, a guarantee of our
inheritance. God's will is to bless those who trust in Christ so that
others will see and worship the God we serve, to the praise of His
glory (Ephesians 1:11-14).

GOD SPEAKS THROUGH WORD PICTURES

Throughout the Scriptures, God often spoke to His people through parables, visions, and dreams. The Bible is full of metaphors that suggest identical parallels between literal and spiritual subjects. Through these word pictures, God helps us to understand what He wants us to know about Himself, His blessings, and His plans and desires for us.

In the visions given to the Old Testament prophets, such as Ezekiel and Zechariah, God likened His own presence to a vast, life-changing river. From the passages of Scripture written by these prophets, we can see a parallel between the river of life and the anointing of God. God's presence brings healing and security in the midst of trouble. His anointing produces joy and gladness in the midst of difficulties (Ezekiel 47:8-9,12 and Psalm 46).

Bible prophecy declares that someday, God's river of life will literally flow from Jerusalem (Zechariah 14:4-8). But even today, God's river of life flows from the Holy Spirit into our spirits to create life within us so that we can be blessed and be a blessing to others.

Zechariah prophesied of the coming day of the Lord, when Satan will gather all the nations to Jerusalem to fight against it. Then, God Himself will fight against those nations. The Word says that He will stand on the Mount of Olives, breaking it in two so that half of it falls to the north and half to the south. On that day, living waters shall go out from Jerusalem, half to the Dead Sea on the east and half to the Mediterranean Sea on the west. Then, the Lord will be king over the whole earth. On that day, there will be one Lord, and His name will be the only name (Zechariah 14:1-9, NIV).

Jerusalem, "the city of the great King" (Matthew 5:35), represents the throne of God, and the river that will one day flow from that city represents the life that flows from God's throne today. Zechariah saw part of the river flow westward into the Mediterranean Sea, and part of it went eastward toward the Dead Sea. When Ezekiel foresaw this same event, he reported that the water in the Dead Sea became fresh when the river flowed into it (Ezekiel 47:9, NIV).

Sadly, many Christians are just like the Dead Sea today. They are lifeless and unable to deliver drinkable, life-giving water to anyone else because they do not release the fresh water they've received from spending time with God. They never offer the water of the Word to others, so their testimony is like stagnant water. They only take in, but never give out. They need a fresh refilling of God's presence to make them life-giving streams that can reach others with His abundant life.

God showed Ezekiel the picture of a time ahead of him—a time when a great river would bring life to those who lived beside it—a time in which I believe we are now living. I believe we are living in a season in which we Christians will continue to bear fruit, because God's river of life is flowing through us. No longer will we suffer endless dry seasons where there is no fruit from our labors.

Through Joel, God Himself prophesied of this outpouring of His Holy Spirit, saying:

> *And it shall come to pass afterward that I will pour out*
> *My Spirit on all flesh; your sons and your daughters shall*
> *prophesy, your old men shall dream dreams, your young men*
> *shall see visions. And also on My menservants and on My*
> *maidservants I will pour out My Spirit in those days.*
> —Joel 2:28-29 (NKJV)

In Joel 3, Joel also prophesied of God's fountain of life:

*And it will come to pass in that day that the mountains shall
drip with new wine, the hills shall flow with milk, and all the
brooks of Judah shall be flooded with water; a fountain shall flow
from the house of the Lord and water the Valley of Acacias.*
—Joel 3:18 (NKJV)

Several hundred years after the prophets wrote of their visions
of God's river, and after every sickness and disease that mankind
endures on this earth, God provided a remedy. God sent His one and
only Son, Jesus Christ, into the world to save the world and bring His
healing and freedom into our lives. Psalmists sang of God's river. The
apostle John received a vision of this river of life during his revelation
of Jesus Christ:

*And he showed me a pure river of water of life, clear as crystal,
proceeding from the throne of God and of the Lamb. In the
middle of its street, and on either side of the river, was the tree
of life, which bore twelve fruits, each tree yielding its fruit every
month. The leaves of the tree were for the healing of the nations.
And there shall be no more curse, but the throne of God and of
the Lamb shall be in it, and His servants shall serve Him.*
—Revelation 22:1-3 (NKJV)

We are entering into a time in history when God desires to pour out
His Spirit on His people, like a great river that is too vast to cross, so
that we can give His healing fruit to the nations and turn their faith to
Him. God has provided for everything that humanity needs. Scientists
have already discovered many natural medicines made from plants of
the earth. It is my opinion that, for every sickness and disease mankind
faces on this earth, God has provided a remedy in the fruit, vegetation,
plants, trees, and leaves that inhabit it. There is healing in the foods that
God created for us to eat.

I also believe that every emotional need mankind has in the spirit realm can find its answer in someone whose life source is from God. The testimony of their good life will point people to Jesus Christ.

JESUS IS COMING AGAIN SOON

Jesus testified to the churches of His return, saying:

> "And behold, I am coming quickly, and My reward is with Me, to give to every one according to his work. I am the Alpha and the Omega, the Beginning and the End, the First and the Last." Blessed are those who do His commandments, that they may have the right to the tree of life, and may enter through the gates into the city. But outside are dogs and sorcerers and sexually immoral and murderers and idolaters, and whoever loves and practices a lie. "I, Jesus, have sent My angel to testify to you these things in the churches. I am the Root and the Offspring of David, the Bright and Morning Star." And the Spirit and the bride say, "Come!" And let him who hears say, "Come!" And let him who thirsts come. Whoever desires, let him take the water of life freely.
> —Revelation 22:12-17, NKJV

God is releasing power through the indwelling presence of the Holy Spirit in His people to heal the nations in preparation for the return of Christ. He is releasing His anointing for a purpose: to win souls. I believe His people are praying more now than at any other time in the history of the church. People are reaching beyond racial, gender, and denominational divides more than at any other moment in church history. We realize we need each other. The church is bearing fruit in a way that we have never seen. The long-awaited harvest of souls is happening.

Mission outreach is not denominational. It is not about an individual man or woman. Many are reporting that, every day, thousands of people throughout the world are accepting Christ as their Savior. We will continue to see an unprecedented harvest of people making decisions to serve Christ. This revival is directly connected to the promised out-pouring of God's Spirit, and the desire of individuals to get into His refreshing waters of life. This vast river of blessing is not denomina-tional. This river is not a mere ministry. This river is not about an indi-vidual man or woman. God is releasing His anointing to save people so they can spend eternity in His presence.

HOW DEEP WILL YOU ENTER INTO THE RIVER?

In this exciting move of God, we can stand on the riverbank and watch, or we can throw ourselves into the flow of God's abundant blessings. We will determine how much fruit we bear by whether or not we choose to abide in the presence of God's abundant blessings. We will determine the size of the harvest we gather for the Lord by the intensity of our direct pursuit of God Himself. We can surrender to waters too deep to stand in, or we can remain in control at the shallow edge. The choice is ours. Every day, we choose how far we are willing to step into the presence of God.

In the early days of our pursuit of God, we may have enjoyed times when we could feel God's presence everywhere we went. It may have seemed that we were "bumping into His blessings" every day. If we wake up one morning and don't feel God's presence, it isn't because He has left; it is because we have stopped looking for Him—we have given up our pursuit of Him.

God is not going to let us get used to just "bumping into Him." He wants to teach us how to flow in His Spirit. When we flow with whatever the Holy Spirit leads us to do, and give ourselves over to Him completely, we enjoy going deeper into the river of His blessings, where we find abundant life. The swim becomes easier in the deeper waters because the power of the river carries us where God wants us to go. Jumping in is all that is required. We enter this river through worshiping God truthfully, with our whole heart.

We won't get into this river any other way. We won't get into the presence of God merely through intellectual ascent. We need to launch out. Jesus said, "But the hour is coming, and now is, when the true worshipers will worship the Father in spirit and truth; for the Father is seeking such to worship Him" (John 4:23, NKJV).

God's river of life has a flow that we can enjoy if we don't resist it and try to swim against its current. If we are facing troubles, we need to get deeper into the river. When everything seems to be breaking loose around us, we need to launch out deeper into the presence of God. No matter what we are struggling against, the answer is to pursue God more strongly.

Perhaps you have already waded out to God in water that is ankle-deep, then to your waist, but the fact is that you have not trusted your entire being to the Lord if both your feet are still on the bottom. At waist-level, you can be half in and half out, just squatting down to give the appearance of being in deep water when, in truth, you are not. Being waist-deep will not bring the abundant blessings that await you in the deeper water. If things are not going the way you want them to go, you can easily pop right back up and stand on your own two feet instead of trusting your entire being to God.

But if you launch out to where the water is too deep to stand, you will finally get to the place of totally depending on God to take you wherever the flow of His blessings may lead. I encourage you to get into the river of life where it is too deep to stand. Get into the flow where you are no longer in control, but are completely dependent on God.

Follow the metaphor of the river. Follow this analogy the Lord has used to illustrate complete surrender to Him. Pursue God until you have moved into the deep part of the water that is full of life. Give up control so that God can make you a fisher of men and move you to a place that is full of fish ready to be caught for Him.

God's anointing isn't just for us to enjoy. He anoints His people so that we can bless others who don't know Him as well as we do. When we are in the flow of the Holy Spirit, He may carry us into a room filled with despair, but He will anoint us to bring peace to everyone in that room, simply because His presence is with us. The anointing of His Spirit in us will bring life to any situation.

Are you in God's flow of blessing now? When you walk into a room filled with contention, do you bring in peace, or do you add to the confusion? Are people excited to see you, or do they try to escape when you walk in? If you are in the flow of God's blessings, you will be anointed to carry His peace. You will be like light in a darkened room.

God has so much to give His people, but we do many things to hinder the flow of His anointing from reaching us and flowing through us to others. God wants to move in our lives because the "hour is coming, and now is" when true worshippers will worship Him in spirit and in truth. When we lift His name in worship, people will see and know that He is God. Just as the river that Ezekiel saw was filled with many kinds of fish, so will our harvest of souls be filled with many kinds of people. God is rescuing people out of every nation, every tribe, every kindred, and every tongue. He is refreshing His people to make us as streams of fresh water to pour out into the dry lands. If we will pursue God and move into the deeper water, He will anoint us to carry His abundant life to everyone we touch.

The greatest miracle of all is the fact that God took our trespasses and sins and saved us from the penalty of death. He took our old, worn-out, good-for-nothing lives and transformed them through the awesome blood of Jesus into glorious, new, fulfilling, and everlasting lives. Because we believe in Jesus Christ, we will not perish (John 3:16). God takes us when we look like grub worms and wraps us in His cocoon of love until we emerge as graceful butterflies. Through the flow of His power, we are made new. He brings abundant life to us, He heals us, and He increases our ministries for the harvest of souls who still need to hear the good news of the gospel. All believers are called to be witnesses of His grace and power. Through our thoughts, words, and deeds, we either help or hinder His flow of blessing in our lives, and thus brighten or dull our ability to testify of His mercy and goodness.

God wants all of us to flow in His anointing. One style of ministry alone is not going to reach everybody who still needs to hear the gospel of Jesus Christ. We can choose to flow with God's anointing and become a stream from His life-giving river, or we can remain as a stagnant marsh. Ezekiel saw this analogy in his vision of the Lord:

He said to me, "Son of man, have you seen this?" Then he brought me and returned me to the bank of the river. When I returned, there, along the bank of the river, were very many trees on one side and the other. Then he said to me: "This water flows toward the eastern region, goes down into the valley, and enters the sea. When it reaches the sea, its waters are healed. And it shall be that every living thing that moves, wherever the rivers go, will live. There will be a very great multitude of fish, because these waters go there; for they will be healed, and everything will live wherever the river goes. It shall be that fishermen will stand by it from En Gedi to En Eglaim; they will be places for spreading their nets. Their fish will be of the same kinds as the fish of the Great Sea, exceedingly many. But its swamps and marshes will not be healed; they will be given over to salt."
—Ezekiel 47:6-11, NKJV

If we reject the flow of God, we position ourselves in that dangerous place. We will become as the lifeless swamplands in Ezekiel's vision. Swamplands and marshes had water flowing into them at one point in time, but because there was no outlet into new fields, the water became stagnant and polluted. Would you rather be a fresh, running stream of living water, or a marsh filled with fetid saltwater?

The swamps and marshes in Ezekiel's vision represent individuals or church families who, at one time, had the source of God's anointing flowing into them, but who didn't remain in God's flow when the river of His anointing made a turn. They enjoyed the flow of His power when He was moving a certain way, but when God wanted to move them in a new direction, they weren't willing to allow Him to redirect their course. Though God Himself is unchangeable in His promises, He continues to make changes in us throughout the seasons of our lives. If we resist His move, we will become as a swampland when He diverts His course to reach new harvest fields of souls.

> We cannot keep going our own way if we want to be a part of the great work God is doing on the earth today. We need to humble ourselves and truthfully worship God.

We can help or hinder the flow of the anointing of God through us. If we choose to harbor offense, bitterness, anger, or unforgiveness, we will hinder the flow of God's anointing in our lives. If we choose to gossip, lie, steal, or slander others, we will hinder the work that God wants to do through us. If we willfully choose to do what His Word clearly tells us not to do, we will block the flow of His power to bless us.

Ultimately, we will be left in the swamps and marshes if we walk back to shore when God's river of life turns away from the direction we want to go. If we don't abide in God, we will be separated from His source of healing and provision.

We cannot keep going our own way if we want to be a part of the great work God is doing on the earth today. We need to humble ourselves and truthfully worship God. We block the flow of God into our lives when we refuse to do what the Bible says we should do. But if we worship God, He will get to us what we need to have, and He will do to us and through us what needs to be done.

CHAPTER NINE

OPENING THE DOOR

"Behold, I stand at the door and knock. If anyone hears My voice and opens the door, I will come in to him and dine with him, and he with Me. To him who overcomes I will grant to sit with Me on My throne, as I also overcame and sat down with My Father on His throne. He who has an ear, let him hear what the Spirit says to the churches."
—Revelation 3:20-22 (NKJV)

One of the more challenging portions of Scripture for me is found in the last book of the Bible, The Book of Revelation, chapter 3 verses 20-22. The picture of Jesus, the Lord of the Church, standing at the door of His church and knocking has always intrigued me. I'm sure you've seen the twentieth-century painting, *The Light of the World* by William Holman Hunt (1827-1910), who began painting his now-famous picture at the age of 21 and finished it when he was 29.

Jesus is depicted as standing at the door of His church, a lantern in His hand, knocking and waiting for someone to open up and invite Him in. For the longest time, I thought this was Jesus making a visitation to a lost soul who would invite Him into their lives and be saved. While that is a possibility, I believe when we look at these verses contextually, we see that Jesus is standing at the door of His church, knocking and desiring for His people to invite Him in so He can fellowship with us.

> Whichever spirit the enemy has used to attack you or work through you to stop God's forward progress in your life, it is time to shut the door on the enemy and open the door of your life to the Lord of the Church.

As we come to the end of our journey of overcoming spirits that hinder the flow of the presence of God in our lives, we also must understand the need for local churches to open up to the flow of His presence again. Too many churches are being led by pastors who have shut themselves off from the very Person that can help and *wants* to help them most. It's my prayer that this book has challenged you to open yourself up again to the possibilities of God. Whichever spirit the enemy has used to attack you or work through you to stop God's forward progress in your life, it is time to shut the door on the enemy and open the door of your life to the Lord of the Church.

ENDING AT THE BEGINNING

I will never forget the day I realized I did not have to be dominated by these spirits that were plaguing my ministry, my marriage, and my church. It was like someone opened a window that allowed a breeze of fresh air to come in and clean out all the stale air of tradition. When I finally understood that the finished work of Jesus Christ at Calvary was enough, I felt like the proverbial bird that had been set free. No longer did I have to look to a man or a system to free me. God did that for me at Calvary over 2,000 years ago.

The only thing I needed to do was learn how to open myself up again to God's presence and appropriate His finished work in my life. I thank God for the men and women who are used by God in the deliverance ministry, but too many of them have been guilty of adding to what God has already done through His Son, Jesus. They cloak it in religious rituals and objects. Instead of setting people free, they create a dependency on themselves. Thus, the person looks to this man or woman for "their word" to get them through their situation. The sad truth is far more people than we can imagine are in the deliverance ministry and do not even see that they are guilty of building a following around their gifts. Beware, for they are becoming wolves in sheep's clothing and drawing the hearts of His people from Him to them.

Too many in the church are looking to someone else before they look to God. They haven't been taught to stand on their own feet, spiritually speaking, and to learn to hear from God for themselves in their unique situation. Let me state clearly: I am not saying it's wrong to look to others for help—seeking godly counsel is a biblical way to move forward. But we almost always go to someone first before we go to God. Go to God and humble yourself in His presence. Acknowledge that you need His help, and let Him guide you to His best solution for finding and receiving that help. I don't believe this is an overstatement: we ought to be going to God daily, many times a day, and acknowledging that we need His help.

In my more than forty-five years of ministry, I've learned that walking free from the control of hindering spirits is easier than many have made it seem. It really boils down to knowing the God you say you serve, in an intimate and personal way, and knowing who you are in Christ because of His finished work at Calvary and the empty tomb! This precious truth is so overlooked in many churches and ministries. If you don't know the God you serve and know who you are in Christ, it will be impossible to know what is truly right and wrong.

If you're not a Christ-follower and you're reading these truths, it is imperative you begin by accepting Jesus as your Savior and Lord. Acknowledge right now that you are a sinner and you need a Savior. Believe that Jesus Christ is the Son of God sent to save you. That simple acknowledgement of your belief will set you on the path to a full life in Christ.

HOW TO APPROPRIATE THE TRUTHS IN THIS BOOK

First, as a Christ-follower, know the truth concerning the devil: he is a defeated foe who has no power in or over us except the power we give him through fear, doubt, unbelief, and selfishness. This truth was made so plain to me years ago when I believed the apostle Paul's teaching about the finished work of Jesus and the true, present state of the enemy in my life—this truth is found in Colossians 2:8-15 (NIV):

See to it that no one takes you captive through hollow and deceptive philosophy, which depends on human tradition and the elemental spiritual forces of this world rather than on Christ. For in Christ all the fullness of the Deity lives in bodily form, and in Christ you have been brought to fullness. He is the head over every power and authority. In him you were also circumcised with a circumcision not performed by human hands. Your whole self ruled by the flesh was put off when you were circumcised by Christ, having been buried with him in baptism, in which you were also raised with him through your faith in the working of God, who raised him from the dead. When you were dead in your sins and in the uncircumcision of your flesh, God made you alive with Christ. He forgave us all our sins, having canceled the charge of our legal indebtedness, which stood against us and condemned us; he has taken it away, nailing it to the cross. And having disarmed the powers and authorities, he made a public spectacle of them, triumphing over them by the cross.

The above Scripture, written by Paul under the inspiration of the Holy Spirit, changed my life. Sadly, this powerful truth is greatly misunderstood by so many standing and teaching in the pulpit—and by those sitting and being taught in the pew. If you understand that the blood of Jesus canceled out all the debt against you, then you can begin to conduct your life at a level of freedom that is so refreshing.

Second, trust and yield to God. This sounds so simple, yet why do most of us struggle with truly doing this? Trusting God is so liberating. Just knowing that He cares for me, far more than anyone ever will, should cause me to trust Him. When I yield my way to His way, I will always come out the winner. I love what Solomon instructs his sons to do—and us, for that matter, in Proverbs 3:5-8 (NIV):

> When I yield my way to His way, I will always come out the winner.

Trust in the Lord with all your heart and lean not on your own understanding; in all your ways submit to him, and he will make your paths straight. Do not be wise in your own eyes; fear the Lord and shun evil. This will bring health to your body and nourishment to your bones.

I fully believe that many of you will walk with a new sense of purpose and freedom when you understand that the evil one is defeated, and that God has given you power to live free from the devil's domination. This is a journey, and it will not be over until we finally stand before our Lord. But until then, we can stop the spirits that have hindered the flow of God in our lives, homes, and churches by simply knowing who we are in Christ, by knowing that the devil has already been defeated and has no power over us, and by trusting and yielding our lives and decisions to God and His will.

ABOUT THE AUTHOR

U nder the leadership of Senior Pastor Jim Bolin, Seven Springs Church has grown from less than fifty members to a thriving church touching thousands of lives. Through his journey, God has taught Pastor Bolin many crucial lessons in the development of a ministry.

God revealed to Pastor Bolin seven spirits that hinder God's anointing, presence, and power from flowing freely through the local church. The spirits that can hinder the flow of God's power in your ministry are:

→ Criticism
→ Rebellion
→ Error
→ Disloyalty
→ Manipulation
→ Confusion
→ Legalism

It is urgent that pastors learn to expose these spirits in their congregations in order to unlock the potential to deliver explosive growth and health to the body of Christ.

CPSIA information can be obtained
at www.ICGtesting.com
Printed in the USA
BVHW030456100822
644218BV00003B/8